It's Where *Our* Words *Come* From!

DUSTIN A. WOODS

ISBN 979-8-89243-998-5 (paperback)
ISBN 979-8-89243-999-2 (digital)

Copyright © 2024 by Dustin A. Woods

All rights reserved. No part of this publication may be reproduced, distributed, or transmitted in any form or by any means, including photocopying, recording, or other electronic or mechanical methods without the prior written permission of the publisher. For permission requests, solicit the publisher via the address below.

Christian Faith Publishing
832 Park Avenue
Meadville, PA 16335
www.christianfaithpublishing.com

Printed in the United States of America

To God, the author of life

When you are assembled in the name of the Lord Jesus and my Spirit is present, with the power of our Lord Jesus, you are to deliver this man to Satan for the destruction of the flesh, so that his spirit may be saved in the day of the Lord.
—1 Corinthians 5:4–5

Contents

Chapter 1: Familiarize Yourself with Christ 3
Chapter 2: Christ Revealed..6
Chapter 3: The Spirit Within 9
Chapter 4: Apart from Christ..12
Chapter 5: Joined with the Father 15
Chapter 6: Named Above 18
Chapter 7: Healed by Grace 22
Chapter 8: Before the Beginning 25
Chapter 9: Leading the Way..28
Chapter 10: His Power of Life 31
Chapter 11: Written to Read...37
Chapter 12: Exhort Others..40
Chapter 13: Ransomed to Life 43
Chapter 14: Impartial..46
Chapter 15: Share Jesus...49
Chapter 16: Following After..53
Chapter 17: Creation 56
Chapter 18: From Him 61
Chapter 19: One God 64
Chapter 20: Faith..66
Chapter 21: All Belongs 69
Chapter 22: Forever 73
Chapter 23: Poured Out..78
Chapter 24: Explained 83
Chapter 25: All Things Together 85

Chapter 26: Given To Us 88
Chapter 27: Everyone...91
Chapter 28: From Purpose 94
Chapter 29: Unity..99
Chapter 30: Connected 103
Chapter 31: Remain...107

Prologue

*Your boasting is not good. Do you not know
that a little leaven leavens the whole lump?*
—1 Corinthians 5:6

*How then should we live? Live
celebrating in Christ who alone is this
bread of sincerity and truth.*
—1 Corinthians 5:8

In that day, declares the Lord *of hosts, the peg that
was fastened in a secure place will give way, and it
will be cut down and fall, and the load that was
on it will be cut off, for the* Lord *has spoken.*
—Isaiah 22:25

What then is your trust in? Once that to what you have put all your weight upon is removed, what then remains?

When all else is gone, Christ is joined to the Father.

We better pray before we begin:

Lord of hosts, who has secured our salvation in Christ, be with us now. Set our minds and souls upon these words of Yours so we may become like Christ. Load our beings with good and wholesome things of life. Speak to us so that we may believe this day in Christ's name. Amen.

Chapter 1

Familiarize Yourself with Christ

If they would have known who He was, those who did so would not have crucified the Lord of glory and still His Word remains:

> What no eye has seen, nor ear heard, nor the heart of man imagined, what God has prepared for those who love Him. (1 Corinthians 2:9)

Before Christ suffered, this world was informed of who He was and what would make Him known, and yet Christ, the olive tree, was beaten for us (Isaiah 24:13 ESV). To this day, long after Christ's ascension into the clouds, our ears hear voices giving praise to the One who is worthy, for "from the ends of the earth we hear songs of praise, of glory to the Righteous One" (Isaiah 24:16 ESV). Today, the same spirit that raised Christ is the same voice calling all who will believe into fellowship with Him (1 Corinthians 1:9 ESV).

Christ was not defeated; His body triumphed over what was intended to be His end. Believers then, such as before His crucifixion, assemble under and within their sovereign Lord Jesus's Spirit When servants of Christ are together, though it might not seem as a loving act of bestowing blessings to one another. For some, at times, what is needed is to deliver a sinful soul who claims to be wise over, even to Satan, that the outcome may be to improve their faith by putting an end to their idolatry (1 Corinthians 5:4–5 ESV).

With the testimony about Christ confirmed among those who believe, what must continue is the teaching of who Christ's Word says He is (1 Corinthians 1:6 ESV). Time is needed for the restoration of a soul to occur. For a person did not get to be who they have become overnight. Waiting in sustained fellowship with other believers under the supremacy of Christ renews a soul (1 Corinthians 1:7–9 ESV). In His Word with other Christians, all are united in the same mind, the reasoning of Christ (1 Corinthians 1:10 ESV).

As Jesus taught in preaching, you who believe do likewise. Preach the gospel (1 Corinthians 1:17 ESV). For in hearing the gospel, a person's soul is attached to the sustainer of life. The gospel to us who are being saved is the power of God, for it is written of the Lord:

> I will destroy the wisdom of the wise, and
> the discernment of the discerning I will thwart.
> (1 Corinthians 1:19)

To explaining the gospel, God saves men with men (1 Corinthians 1:21 ESV). The Father saved humanity with a man. This man is Christ the power of God and the wisdom of God in a person (1 Corinthians 1:24 ESV).

Since the beginning, because of the Father, you are in Christ Jesus (1 Corinthians 1:30 ESV). Now in belonging to Christ the wisdom of God, who is righteous is sanctifying believers and further redeeming His disciples by His Spirit (1 Corinthians 1:30 ESV). All who claim Jesus as Lord remain quiet, for their works are futile apart from Jesus. Live then so that others may experience Christ alive within them, as it is written, "Let the one who boasts, boast in the Lord" (1 Corinthians 1:31 ESV).

The command

> Do not love the world or the things in the
> world. If anyone loves the world, the love of the

Father is not in him. For all that is in the world—the desires of the flesh and the desires of the eyes and pride of life—is not from the Father but is from the world. And the world is passing away along with its desires, but whoever does the will of God abides forever. (1 John 2:15–17 ESV)

Prayer

Father of the One who sets up salvation, we believe this day in Christ (Isaiah 26:1 ESV). Keep the gates of heaven open as our desire is to enter your kingdom (Isaiah 26:2, 8 ESV). Our souls yearn for your Spirit to guide us (Isaiah 26:9 ESV). So lead us on the path of righteousness by your Spirit of grace. Amen (Isaiah 26:7 ESV).

Chapter 2

Christ Revealed

*For the Word of the cross is folly to those
who are perishing, but to us who are
being saved it is the power of God.*
—1 Corinthians 1:18

Be still before the Lord as He unveils the hidden mysteries of creation to us (Isaiah 23:2 ESV). Humility begins with proclaiming to others the testimony of God's Word from the source of sincerity (1 Corinthians 2:1 ESV). Giving God the glory is not in the words from humanity but from Christ, the spokesman of heaven, the giver of life, and the incarnate Son of God (1 Corinthians 2:1 ESV).

With Christ as our advocate, the simplicity of the kingdom of heaven resides within Christ crucified, known as the gospel message of Jesus Christ (1 Corinthians 2:2 ESV).

The Bible teaches us to become a disciple of Christ, be ashamed of your sin, then be raised in the ways of the Lord by the knowledge of wisdom (Isaiah 23:4 ESV). In other words, be broken by the knowledge of what you have become, who God is, the difference between each of you, and yet God invites us to join Him as followers of His Son the Christ (1 Corinthians 2:3 ESV). Humility is realizing that, in all the efforts of life, we are helpless in entering salvation without

Christ. Our weakness is what God uses to teach us how pointless our ways without God have become (1 Corinthians 2:3 ESV).

This weakness in Christ is a strength of God, an opportunity for His Spirit to first give us understanding of what it is to reverence the Lord—out of fear (1 Corinthians 2:3 ESV). The good fears where our souls tremble before the message about Christ's life (1 Corinthians 2:3–4 ESV). Believers learn how God works out His plans into our lives as *it* says,

> The LORD of hosts has purposed it, to defile the pompous pride of all glory, to dishonor all the honored of the earth (Isaiah 23:9 ESV).

> "All things are lawful," but not all things are helpful. "All things are lawful," but not all things build up (1 Corinthians 10:23 ESV).

> He has stretched out his hand over the sea; he has shaken the kingdoms; the LORD has given command concerning Canaan to destroy its strongholds (Isaiah 23:11 ESV).

What the Lord seeks to accomplish is to remove what binds a person's soul to sin. This is in the Lord taking that to what is within a person, then never allowing the stronghold to enter a person again. This is the conquering power of the living God. Protection remains with those who are joined with God deflecting the attempts of a stronghold that seeks to reclaiming a soul.

In saying this, the message of Christ is lived out in the messengers of the kingdom of heaven in the here and in the now (1 Corinthians 2:4 ESV). For we who believe learn we are nothing without the Word of God, the power of the Holy Spirit; and without Christ forgiving us, we would be eternally separated from the kingdom where our creator resides. Therefore, our lives in Christ are transformed by the Holy Spirit demonstrating His own power in our words and actions to one another (1 Corinthians 2:4 ESV).

Why does God work this way?

As we are told, God operates according to His own good purposes and plans. God remains faithful and obedient to His own Word. God takes control of our souls so that we remain connected with Him by His Spirit (1 Corinthians 2:5 ESV). God wants us to know that our faith has nothing to do with us; rather, God seeks for His Word to rest in our beings so that our minds may be renewed daily, not from the wisdom of others but from His Spirit joining us to the all-powerful One (1 Corinthians 2:5 ESV).

Prayer

God of merciful might, dominion, and authority, remove what keeps us from serving you today. Do in our lives what pleases your Spirit; may we be obedient to the leading of your Word this day. Teach us how to abide in your ways so that your Holy Spirit may have access to our souls. Show us what may occur immediately in surrendering to your will, in Christ's name. Defeat strongholds, remove unwanted harmful spirits that are near us, and reset our lives by your Spirit of grace. We ask in Jesus's name. Amen.

Chapter 3

The Spirit Within

What God seeks to tell you is that the anointing from the Holy Spirit lives in you (1 John 2:27 ESV). All you need is a want to read His Word as God is constrained to His own Word; He yearns to teach you directly (1 John 2:27 ESV)!

What then is hindering the Spirit from revealing truth is more so a who than a what. As the deceiver, the Antichrist, that ancient serpent of old, spreads lies, you who believe seek after God (1 John 2:22 ESV).

How to gain maturity by yourself with the ability to impart wisdom to others is accessible to those who God has predestined long ago (1 Corinthians 2:6–7 ESV). This sharing of the gospel, though attainable from God to any believer, is best displayed among two or more believers (1 Corinthians 2:6 ESV).

For if you love those who love you, how is God glorified (Luke 6:32 ESV)? Even those sinners who refuse Christ show mercy to others (Luke 6:32 ESV). Those without Christ live with a sense of using others for their own good. Where believers are to differ is in a love that blesses those who intentionally shame and despise Christ (Luke 6:27 ESV). Believers are to allow others to keep what is rightfully theirs (Luke 6:29–30 ESV).

Expect nothing in return for living at peace with others (Luke 6:35 ESV). A day is approaching that far outweighs our humanity as *it* says:

> What no eye has seen, nor ear heard, nor the heart of man imagined, what God has prepared for those who love Him! 1 Corinthians 2:9

Our Lord on His cross sought to teach us to love those who persecute and even crucify you, for Jesus said, while nailed to His cross, "Father, forgive these who are unaware of what they are doing, for their souls are overwhelmed by the evil one" (Luke 23:34 ESV).

Would you pray for those who are yet to receive Christ?

These things of loving and praying for one another are what pleases our Lord (1 Corinthians 2:10 ESV). Helping others always begins with ourselves. Each person may ask the Holy Spirit to bring forth what is keeping them from maturing in godliness (1 Corinthians 2:10 ESV). What might be unknown to you is most certainly known by God, for His Spirit searches the depths of our souls, not to condemn us but to save us (1 Corinthians 2:10; John 3:17 ESV).

The Spirit of God is love, for the Father gave Jesus His only Son for our inheritance into everlasting life (John 3:16 ESV).

Faith in Christ is the gospel!

Don't wait till tomorrow; believe in Christ at once, for you are currently nailed to your sins of condemnation before a righteous God (Luke 23:40–43).

Have you heard what Christ said to the man who decided to ask Christ into His life? Jesus said to a criminal, "Truly, I say to you, today you will be with me in paradise" (Luke 23:43 ESV).

Thought to consider

Lord, my life until this day has mostly been lived for me. There is no blank needed in the above consideration of my soul.

I am selfish, yet I want to give.

IT'S WHERE OUR WORDS COME FROM!

I think I know what is best for my life, while You alone are wise. Reform how I live into the likeness of how Christ lives. Connect my thoughts with Your word of truth. Strengthen me to pick up my Bible and to read at once. In Christ's name. Amen.

Chapter 4

Apart from Christ

For this is a people without discernment.
—Isaiah 27:11

The things taught to us in the Word of God are best learned from the Holy Spirit (1 Corinthians 2:10 ESV). These inexplainable in human terms, these what the Spirit searches of God, are made known to those who ask for truth to be revealed to them (1 Corinthians 2:10 ESV).

For all who began in the natural condition of being alive yet unable to comprehend the Words of God are becoming as those who set their faith in Christ being taught the truth (1 Corinthians 2:14 ESV). Then as a believer, the ways of God are explained effortlessly from Scripture by Him who sent Christ to teach us—the Helper (1 Corinthians 3:14 ESV). Jesus told His remaining eleven disciples after His crucifixion moments before His ascension into heaven to stay (Luke 24:44–49 ESV).

This Spirit of truth within the risen Savior brought into words the disciples, words anointed by the Holy Spirit, the fulfillment of what had just occurred (Luke 24:44–45 ESV).

With Christ's Spirit, believers live with comfort in their souls (Luke 24:36 ESV). How the Holy Spirit works in discerning the Word for us is that the Holy Spirit and the Father and the Son are one (John 16:4–15 ESV). The thoughts that are the mind of the Father share all things with the mind of Him—our Helper, the Holy Spirit (1 Corinthians 2:11 ESV).

As we are told

Comprehension of God belongs to those who are in fellowship in the Holy Spirit, as "no one comprehends the thoughts of God except the Spirit of God" (1 Corinthians 2:11 ESV).

God wants for all people to gain discernment of His kingdom; confirmation of this is in Christ and the Father is sending the Helper to instruct us in a spiritual voice (Luke 2:12–13 ESV). Permission into heaven begins with accepting Christ as your Lord and Savior. What was unknown to you is now being made into plausible thoughts—as the point of creation.

To whom does the Holy Spirit interpret spiritual truths (1 Corinthians 2:13 ESV)? To those who hear His voice. In part, we find out that what is known by God is confirmed in His Word, imparted to us by His Spirit (1 Corinthians 2:13 ESV).

See what kind of love the Father has given to us who believe that we should be called children of God, and because of Christ's sacrifice, since God gave us His Spirit, we are forgiven and now taught truth (1 John 3:1 ESV). In an instant, faith in Christ transforms a life spent devoted to one mindset, in a moment of grace knowing Him who has existed before this world was made (1 John 3:1 ESV). The Holy Spirit appears within our minds with whom God is refashioning us after, His Son (1 John 3:1 ESV).

This life we live now is all directed toward our eternal life that is to follow (1 John 3:2 ESV). Words in the Bible tell us, "What we will become is yet to be shown to us fully" (1 John 3:2 ESV). What we instead comprehend is who we know greater than us is Christ (1 John 3:2 ESV). In part, as Christ was sent to us, we live now in this present condition waiting for His return (1 John 3:2 ESV).

Therefore, we who believe inherit this—that Christ has appeared in the form of human likeness, that His Spirit has been freely given to all who receive Jesus so we live in a heightened anticipation of

Christ's second coming. For now, after being given the Holy Spirit, we know when His presence is among and present with us (1 John 3:2 ESV).

What is left for everyone who hopes in Christ is a life of being sanctified by the washing of the Spirit and by the Word of God (1 John 3:3 ESV).

Creator of life, we want to be pure as You, Lord, are pure (1 John 3:3 ESV). Cleanse our minds, souls, and beings with truth this day, in Christ's name, would You do so now.

Chapter 5

JOINED WITH THE FATHER

Love is from God.
—1 John 4:7 ESV

Our spiritual birth binds our minds to the thoughts of Christ (Philippians 2:12–18; 1 John 4:7 ESV). This imputed truth is how the Lord will and does manifest Himself to us (John 14:22 ESV). "It" imputed truth from the Father is only transferred from God the Father by His Holy Spirit to believers and not to the world—nonbelievers (John 14:22 ESV). For what is known by the Spirit is revealed to those who have faith that God is the Creator, that His Son Jesus is our Savior and Redeemer. All things pertaining to godliness and life then are taught not to unrepentant souls but to those who trust what the Spirit teaches them in their minds and souls, which is indeed imputed truth directly from the Father.

So we who believe rejoice in how God so chooses to work out His will into our lives (Philippians 2:17 ESV). For our benefit is to know the Lord for His good pleasure is to instruct us (Philippians 2:13 ESV).

The Helper is the Spirit who will bring to remembrance the former things of God (John 14:16, 26 ESV). This attribute of God being love that is the greatest of all enables this fellowship in the Spirit (1 Corinthians 13:13; John 14:15 ESV).

Our purpose

Do as Christ; do as the Father has commanded. Do this so that the world may know that I, Jesus, love the Father (John 14:31 ESV). Obey at all times when Christ is present or when He is with the Father. Little children, from now on, live in accordance with what Scripture teaches and what the Helper reveals (Philippians 2:12; 1 John 3:7 ESV). For the Helper who has been with Christ from the beginning is building upon Christ (1 Corinthians 3:10 ESV). Christ laid the foundation in Zion, the city of refuge, beginning with Christ, the only tested stone, who is the sure structure of truth (Isaiah 28:16 ESV).

In these present days, Christ is setting His dominion within us, so as believers, we wait in eager anticipation as the Holy Spirit makes known to us that Christ is already crowned in glory (Isaiah 28:5 ESV).

Who, then, are we to God if Christ is complete? We are His people who are a diadem of beauty as the remaining remnant to build upon what God the Father began with Christ (Isaiah 28:5 ESV). What greater reason to find the purpose of life than to abide in Christ for the Spirit seeks to teach us the knowledge of the Lord (Isaiah 28:9 ESV)? Who has given the Holy Spirit authority?

This imputed truth to us needs only faith, for He the Helper is the instructor of life (Isaiah 28:26 ESV). As we believe, we receive who the Father has entrusted to us being His own Spirit, as the Helper is the voice of reason (Isaiah 28:16 ESV).

What's next?

In all of these things, the Spirit guides us from unknowing the word of grace as infants who need to be fed a little at a time to be fully capable followers of Christ who, with the Word of God and the instructions from the Helper, will read, grow, and mature into the likeness of Christ (1 Corinthians 3:1–2 ESV).

Christ is our example of what God can achieve in the life of a mere human, for Christ is the perfection of life living within the only

Son of God, Jesus, who is far beyond a mere human (1 Corinthians 3:9 ESV). What our Lord and King shares with us in our human likeness is that He, such as every person born, began this nurturing with a small portion of God at a time (1 Corinthians 3:1–9 ESV).

Where Christ is unlike any before or after Him, where He differs, even from the Helper, is that Christ surpasses all of humanity; He is beyond angels and is equal to yet different from the Holy Spirit. Christ was obedient on what the Word taught Him as He lived a sinless life in dependance of the will of the Father.

While after Christ's ascension, He has now given us His Spirit so that where we are, God is with us (John 14:15–16, 26 ESV). Christ is building upon "it" imputed truth given to us from His own Spirit (1 Corinthians 3:10 ESV).

Beloved, if God so loved us, we also ought to love one another (1 John 4:11 ESV). We love because He first loved us (1 John 4:19 ESV).

Chapter 6

NAMED ABOVE

For the Father is greater than I.
—John 14:28

Above are humble words from the One who conquered death. Add year to year, grace upon grace, Christ lives in your soul (Isaiah 29:1 ESV). In an instant, the LORD of hosts will visit you; in your soul this will occur as a vision of the LORD from the Holy Spirit (Isaiah 29:5–7 ESV).

Contentment is given to you by God (Isaiah 29:8 ESV). Be astonished in your soul by what the Holy Spirit will open to you (Isaiah 29:9, 11 ESV). Once, though spiritually closed, in mercy this Book of Life is now opened to you as your eyes ponder upon the truth (Isaiah 29:11–12 ESV).

Christ is telling you now before it takes place that your soul is transformed by His Spirit in an instant (John 14:28–29; Isaiah 29:5 ESV).

Who has the authority to break the seal of the Book of Life? "Who is worthy to open the scroll and break its Seals?" Revelation 5:2

Christ is the king of heaven who instantly makes all things new; Christ is worthy to open His Word to you (Isaiah 29:11–12; Revelation 5:1–6:1 ESV). Why is Christ the only One who may break the seal of eternal life for us? For He alone is the Son of God,

Christ is the blameless spotless Lamb of God that takes away the sins of your life (Revelation 5:6 ESV).

What is promised by the Father in Christ to us who believe is Christ will keep us from eternal condemnation (Revelation 3:10–11 ESV). Though we think in our lives it is us who have endured for so long, it is our Creator who is and has patiently been waiting (Revelation 3:10–11 ESV), waiting for us to believe and imploring us to wait until we receive His Word into our beings so we may live in His Word as His Word is the source of all things.

God longs for all to receive what appeared to us as mercy, in the person of Jesus, who keeps us from the condemnation of our sins (1 John 3:4–6 ESV). So we who trust in Christ live dependent on Him, and yet the Father is even greater than the Son (John 14:28 ESV). Obedience to God's commands bring us to the Father while those who make a practice of sinning after receiving knowledge of Christ no longer have Christ's grace to remove their sins (1 John 3:4 ESV).

> [For] "You know that He appeared in order to take away sins, and in Him there is no sin."
> 1 John 3:5

Jesus appeared to cleanse us by His death on His cross from our sins (John 19:30 ESV). As Christ takes away the sins of the World, in Him—the Father, the Son, and in the Holy Spirit—there is only holiness (1 John 3:5). Jesus tells us then to forgive others, then we will be forgiven (Luke 6:37 ESV).

Christ gives us His Word to treasure in our souls, then we grow in Christ as we give His Word to others (Luke 6:38 ESV). Jesus yearns for us to lead one another by His divine scriptures (Luke 6:39–40 ESV). Becoming like Christ requires the reading of His Word (Luke 6:40; 1 Corinthians 3:11 ESV).

It is required of Christ's disciples to search the Scriptures for in time as this imputed truth tells us:

> A disciple is not above His teacher, but everyone when he is fully trained will be like his teacher. Luke 6:40

Likewise, since there exists this grace of God, what we have then within our hands is His voice put on paper for us to behold (1 Corinthians 3:10 ESV). Take value in how you tell others of Jesus Christ, for God cares how His Word is shared (1 Corinthians 3:10–11 ESV). There is no hiding our words from one another, for what is within us is disclosed to one another as we speak (1 Corinthians 3:12–13 ESV). How we sort through His Word matters to God, for He gave His Son for His Word to be given to us (1 Corinthians 3:13 ESV).

Speak each word of God in faith as abiding in Christ, is becoming your inheritance (1 Corinthians 3:14 ESV). For Christ suffered His crucifixion that His Word and His Spirit may be given to you (1 Corinthians 3:15 ESV).

In His book, on that day of faith, the Holy One of Israel will make the deaf to hear His Word and the blind to see truth (Isaiah 29:11, 18–19 ESV).

Our Lord has for us in His Scriptures this promise that the deaf shall hear the words of a book (Isaiah 29:18 ESV). Conquering the cross now, Christ promises to fulfill what was written prior to the cross and before His birth, which is what the Holy Spirit is able to do from the source of wisdom. Scripture says without being able to hear sounds, the word of life will be heard, then received not as noise but as divinely inspired by Christ Himself.

For those unable to see the words on the pages in His holy book from their despair sight to perceive in the Spirit is given to the blind (Isaiah 29:18 ESV). No longer will anyone be able to claim the truth of Scripture to be hidden, for Christ removed the seal inviting all to learn from the Helper—the Holy Spirit—the author of life (Isaiah 29:11–12 ESV).

The reason the Son of God appeared was to destroy the works of the devil (1 John 3:8 ESV).

The invitation

Only say the Word, and heaven will be opened to you (Isaiah 29:21 ESV).

Chapter 7

HEALED BY GRACE

The resurrected Christ is for love.
—1 John 4:7

Christ was resurrected so His love would live through us (1 John 4:9 ESV). We live in Christ as Jesus lives within our beings (1 John 4:9 ESV). The Spirit of the living creator is manifested in us, who have Christ (1 John 4:7 ESV).

Christ's claim for us

"But now, thus says the Lord, He who created you, He who has formed you, loves you. As we are told, 'Fear not, for I have redeemed you: I have called you by name, you are mine'" (Isaiah 43:1 ESV).

Jesus knows us exceedingly greater than our name, as He in His name claims us as His own! "Everyone Jesus tells us in His Word, everyone who is called a Christian, called by My name," says Jesus, "is mine" (Isaiah 43:7 ESV).

Everyone—all believers of Christ—created after the image of Christ the Son of the invisible God is made to glorify the Father (Isaiah 43:7 ESV).

Jesus's redemption of our lives began with His resurrection first (Isaiah 43:1–7 ESV). For Christ created humanity, then in our failures and in our sins, Christ showed us the perfect love of the Father in saving us by then resurrecting us from being disconnected to being formed in the likeness of Christ's resurrection (Isaiah 43:1, 7 ESV). Jesus shares with us that wherever we go in this His creation, He will be there among our circumstances (Isaiah 43:2 ESV). Now as offspring in this resurrection of Christ's Spirit indwelling our souls, God will not allow us to be overwhelmed yet further refined as He is making us into the image of Christ (Isaiah 43:2, 5 ESV). Christians are sanctified by the works of Jesus's nail-pierced hands and feet (John 24:39–40 ESV).

> Christians are sanctified by the works of Christ's hands. Isaiah 29:23

Jesus redeemed us. He is sanctifying us, and Christ even gives us His name (Isaiah 29:22, 23 ESV). Christ left this world with those at His cross standing in awe, saying, "Truly this was the Son of God" (Isaiah 29:23; Matthew 27:54 ESV)! Those who are called by His name still, to this day, say, "Truly Jesus is the Son of our Creator" (Matthew 27:54 ESV)!

What is required of disciples of Christ is to be found faithful (1 Corinthians 4:2 ESV). Jesus, in His glorified body after His death and burial and in His eternal condition, appeared to His disciples. As servants and stewards of the Word of God, the disciples must then be obedient as Christ was obedient even unto death on His cross (1 Corinthians 4:1; Matthew 27:50, 28:9 ESV).

Christ's broken body that was given for us is what disciples gather to talk of; it is when disciples of Christ marvel at the works of Jesus's life—that Christ brings peace into our lives (Luke 24:35–41, ESV).

The love of Christ is perfected in His disciples, who abide in Christ, as Christ abides with the Father (1 John 4:12 ESV). The realization of the love of God is by knowing Christ and of His sacrifice, for God loved us in giving us His only Son (1 John 4:11 ESV).

Confidence in this eternal hope of glory is built upon proof of Christ' resurrection as He appeared to His disciples who testify and proclaim, "He is risen!" 1 John 4:14; Luke 24:34

How about you this day? Do you understand that Christ had to rise from the dead to give you eternal life? John 20:10

Speak truth to one another

Again, what the conversations the disciples of Christ speak of are all that Jesus began to do and is doing unto this day (Luke 24:17; John 21:25 ESV).

Chapter 8

BEFORE THE BEGINNING

*This Jesus, delivered up according to the
definite plan and foreknowledge of God.*
—Acts 2:23

God seeing beforehand what we would become and the Father of Christ knowing what we would do to His Son still predestined that He would forgive us.

In our arrogance do we dare tell God, "Look at us," for He sees into our souls and He has compassion for us (Acts 3:4 ESV).

Upon the truth of Christ, the church will be established (John 16:12–15 ESV). How is the church built? Upon Christ's life and His promise that He will send the Holy Spirit (Luke 24:49 ESV). Then as the Lord waits to be gracious to us, we see His mercy toward us in His long-suffering; for in due time, the Lord will exalt Himself to us and in us (Isaiah 30:18 ESV).

It says that the Father will direct our hearts back to His own love for us if we remain faithful to Christ (2 Thessalonians 3:3–5 ESV). Confidence in one another is not from us nor from our own efforts but of God's Word living within us (2 Thessalonians 3:4 ESV). The confirmation of truth from God given to us to read then becomes who we are, so we live as ambassadors of and for Christ (2 Thessalonians 3:4 ESV).

Busyness in the things of God that pertain to eternal life takes hold of the outcome of our choices to strive for excellence as the day of Christ's return is ever approaching (2 Thessalonians 3:11–12 ESV). So we both earn our keep and are kept by this spirit of mercy and loving kindness of grace served to us as unmerited favor from our Lord (2 Thessalonians 3:12 ESV).

Quietly and efficiently, the Holy Spirit leads from the earnings of the kingdom of heaven, where forgiveness is the currency of life perfected (2 Thessalonians 3:12 ESV). For in this letter to humanity from our creator, this Book of Life—known as imputed truth—as our Holy Bible, we find peace in every way, at all times, in what we receive from Christ (2 Thessalonians 3:13–16 ESV).

It is of what is within Christ's written Word to us that, by grace, His divine letter constrains us to obedience (2 Thessalonians 3:17–18 ESV). Quietly making Himself further known to us, His Holy Spirit sets His Word as the motivation for our eternity (2 Thessalonians 3:12 ESV).

The Spirit seeks to show and teach us as He is, whose Father is the purity of life (1 John 3:1–3 ESV). The Helper is connected with the Father, so we may be like Him, a teacher of truth of His Word in this world (1 John 3:2 ESV). In deed and in truth, the love of the Father expounds our hearts with gladness (1 John 3:16–18 ESV). Instructions from Scripture tell us yes to speak truth of the Word to others while then giving ourselves for the improvement of other's souls (1 John 3:18 ESV). Little by little, we gain likeness with Christ as we serve in action of His truth (1 John 3:18 ESV).

> For this is the message that you have heard from the beginning, that we should love one another. 1 John 3:11

The Spirit makes the Father known to us (Luke 6:43 ESV). These words of ours are no longer ours but of the One who was sent to instruct us—the Helper of the Father (Luke 6:43 ESV). Being then transformed from enemies of Christ to now partakers of eternal

IT'S WHERE OUR WORDS COME FROM!

life, the words we say derive out of the abundance of the heart of Christ's mouth (Luke 6:45 ESV).

What is meant of God creating these bodies of ours is of and for the Lord's purposes (1 Corinthians 6:13 ESV).

> Have you not heard? You are not your own but Christ!

Members of Christ validate their lives as raised into sonship of the immortal spirit (1 Corinthians 6:13–18 ESV).

> But he who is joined to the Lord becomes one Spirit with Him! 1 Corinthians 6:17

Lord, allow us then to return to this rest found in the quietness of our Savior (Isaiah 30:15 ESV). Strengthen our trust to live in alliance with Christ's spirit (Isaiah 30:1, 15 ESV). Christ's spirit that breathes with an abundance from the voice of the Father (Isaiah 30:31, 33 ESV). Indeed, the king of heaven is making us ready for heaven (Isaiah 30:33 ESV).

The finality of Christ

Help us to take value of these bodies You, God, have developed into vessels that bestow Your Spirit (1 Corinthians 6:19–20 ESV). Astonish our minds as worthy in Christ to be called as recipients of wisdom. Commit Your Word within us this day and each day for we confess we need You, Lord (1 Corinthians 6:18 ESV).

Chapter 9

LEADING THE WAY

> I am ascending to my Father and your
> Father, to my God and your God.
> —John 20:17

Jesus says that the Father is His God! How much more should we profess God as our creator in the name of Christ! Fill our lungs with the life of Christ to breath out truth into one another (John 20:22 ESV).

Lord let us "receive the Holy Spirit" (John 20:22).

Now concerning the matters of prayer (1 Corinthians 7:1, 5 ESV), pray for self-control to be given to you from God (1 Corinthians 7:5 ESV). Ask Christ to petition the Father not as a concession, a suggested notion but as a command to do what I, the Lord, command (1 Corinthians 7:6 ESV).

For the gift from God to us is of Himself—His Spirit and His Son, both given to us so that all who believe may be "one" (1 Corinthians 7:7 ESV).

Not I but the Lord says that believers are to remain faithful and obedient to Christ among nonbelievers so that the Lord may restore them by the conduct of believers (1 Corinthians 7:12 ESV). For in the end, your cleanliness belongs and is entrusted with Christ who keeps us a wholesome one unto another (1 Corinthians 7:14 ESV).

IT'S WHERE OUR WORDS COME FROM!

Christ consents with the Father on the behalf of those bound in the covenant promise. The Helper remains with us for Christ is faithful on our behalf (1 Corinthians 7:13 ESV).

Therefore, each person is made holy by the works of God (1 Corinthians 7:14 ESV). If any of us are so determined to condemn ourselves into the bondage of eternal separation from God, then let it be so (1 Corinthians 7:15 ESV).

Only let Christ rule your soul, for the condition of your previous life is vanishing away and for the Holy Spirit of Christ is assigned to never leave you but to guide believers who are called by God (1 Corinthians 7:17 ESV). This world needs godly people in all professions of life. Remain then in the condition you were in when you believed while not hindering but allowing the Spirit to exhort your lives as renamed or as developed by Christ (1 Corinthians 7:17 ESV).

Worry not on what your calling is; instead, be concerned about *it*—how you will live for Christ— and be concerned with telling others of the imputed truth, of who your Savior is to you (1 Corinthians 7:21 ESV).

So, believer, condition your habits after Christ as all are one with God (1 Corinthians 7:24 ESV). Are not your worldly troubles the results of sin? Again, believers, conduct all you do as members of the household of faith in accordance with Scripture and live having no dealings with sin, for the light of Christ's life is within whom your freedom belongs (1 Corinthians 7:21 ESV).

There is no division in Christ. If you receive Christ's life in truth, go promote His good order. Value your spouse and "let them marry" who are yet to do so, "it is no sin" to be married (1 Corinthians 7:36-38, ESV). Nothing can restrain the message of salvation; share the freeing power from anxieties to those of divided interest that they may become bond servants of Christ (1 Corinthians 7:32–38 ESV). Willingly submit by conditioning your life after what the Scripture tells us all—that Christ did and began to do in His earthly life (John 20:30–31 ESV).

Woe to those who attempt to satisfy the Lord by falling away from His commands (Isaiah 31:1 ESV). Because His Word went forth, *it* will either sanctify believers or bring disaster to the disobedient (Isaiah 31:2).

God is wise in how His Word deals with our lives (Isaiah 31:2 ESV). The Lord will not call back His Word; instead, He allows what He has intended to be accomplished (Isaiah 31:2 ESV). Those who oppose the household of faith find that their work is an iniquity against the author of life (Isaiah 31:2 ESV).

For ungodly kings are men and not God, their authority is of the flesh that passes away, yet the Word of God is Spirit (Isaiah 31:3 ESV). Find comfort in even the noise and shouts of desperate souls, for they are terrified by the truth of His resurrection (Isaiah 31:3–4 ESV). Christians hear His voice as *it* rescues, protects, and delivers to who will believe in the only One who has made you (Isaiah 31:5–6 ESV).

We realize that we who believe rejoice that our bodies are the fulfillment of where Your Word abides. God, we trust that our souls that reside within these "temples" are the spot where You refine us. As Your Word is sent forth, we ponder upon the life of Christ from Your ancient Word that is remaking and refining us from within our minds and beings that You first created for us. Some flee by hiding themselves from hearing Your Holy Spirit as we, in faith, receive the edification into our souls as the purity of life and godliness. In Christ, intensify our passion to know You, Lord (Isaiah 31:9)!

Chapter 10

His Power of Life

*What I do have I give to you. In the name of
Jesus Christ of Nazareth, rise up and walk!*
—Acts 3:6

We give what Christ in God gave us—this imputed truth that has been made known to us, His path of life (Acts 2:28 ESV).

Unlike His cross, the Word of God is not burdensome (1 John 5:3 ESV). When Christ was asked by His disciples what is the greatest commandment, He replied, Love one another as I have loved you (Matthew 22:34–40 ESV). Let love overcome the disputes held against your inability to forget one another's trespasses and just forgive as I, Jesus, forgave you (1 John 5:4–5 ESV).

Given to us by divine inspiration of the Holy Spirit, the things written of Christ are for those who believe in the name of the Son of God (1 John 5:13 ESV) and that, in faith, you may have eternal life (1 John 5:13 ESV). If you receive the words of the apostles of Christ, you do well while the testimony from Christ of God is greater (1 John 5:9 ESV).

In the beginning of our faith in Christ, belief in the Son of creation is the life of men (1 John 5:11–12 ESV).

From within your heart, mind, and soul, in all faith and belief, may the Spirit give you the utterance to profess this day of Christ as you experience His presence.

It is the Lord. John 21:7

Each time, such as with His disciples, Christ reveals Himself to you; *it* is to strengthen your confidence that the Lord is Christ (John 21:14 ESV). As we open Scripture, the Holy Spirit's heart burns with a passion to instruct us in the truth of the Father (Luke 24:32 ESV).

So we live

By His name, as our faith in the name of the resurrected Christ has brought health into our souls by the presence of His Holy Spirit (Acts 3:16 ESV).

My Lord and my God! John 20:28

Take dominion of my soul and give me life this day, for I believe in the resurrected Christ! It is only because of Christ that you will be saved (1 Corinthians 3:15 ESV), only as through fire! We are Christ's, and Christ is God's, so we believe (1 Corinthians 3:23 ESV).

"Read this" (Isaiah 29:11 ESV): Not only has God given you the ability, He has made His Word part of your being in saying. When men give *it*—imputed truth—to a person from the One who alone can read the heart of the Father, then faith occurs (Isaiah 29:11–12 ESV). What the Father conveys to the Son is that this is the way; walk in it. "My truth I," says the Father, "give to you" (Isaiah 30:12 ESV).

Since Christ joins us to the Spirit, we live out our lives on what is written, for His Words are not beyond human understanding (1 Corinthians 5:6 ESV). Therefore, this Word from the Father is meant to encourage us in; what we receive is to build us up (1 Corinthians 5:14 ESV).

IT'S WHERE OUR WORDS COME FROM!

These things of God are for believers everywhere, given to us that the household of faith may be rooted and grounded in love (1 Corinthians 4:17 ESV). The Christ says, establish My Word in your souls, for I am coming to you soon (1 Corinthians 4:18 ESV).

We ask of you, Jesus, to pray for us (2 Thessalonians 3:1 ESV). Petition to the Father that the Word may speed ahead among us, delivering us from evil men who seek to silence your truth (2 Thessalonians 3:1–2 ESV).

And Still

In all of this

> Jesus did many other signs in the presence of the disciples, which are not written in this book; but these are written so that you may believe that Jesus is the Christ, the Son of God, and that by believing you may have life in His name. John 20:30–31

*And this is the promise that He
made to us—eternal life.*
—1 John 2:25

Chapter 11

Written to Read

Read all what Christ commanded, and the effect of righteousness within you will be peace, for the result of righteousness is a quiet life. Allow the Holy Spirit to accomplish God's will in your life by trusting Him forever, for there remains only a life of interacting with the Holy Spirit (Isaiah 32:17 ESV).

So go do what you want, yet let it be of God!

Make your home with the Lord, for in doing what *it* tells you, His imputed truth is a life of abiding with God and man in a peaceful habitation (Isaiah 32:18 ESV). In the security of His Word, find rest (Isaiah 32:18 ESV). Invite Christ to dwell in your home and within your soul, and you will gain favor with, first, the Lord then next, with man (Isaiah 32:18 ESV).

While you're at it, study His truth given to you in His Word and include prayer in your life (1 Corinthians 7:5 ESV). Devote yourself to prayer, for the Lord your God has called you to peace (1 Corinthians 7:5, 15 ESV).

Be anxious about nothing; rather, find that by reading the Word of God given to you by God Himself. Peace is offered from His text (Philippians 4:7 ESV). God is concerned about you. If it were not so, He would not have given you understanding of His Word (1 Corinthians 12:3 ESV). In all that man does to gain dominion of this world, do you think for a moment that the birds of the air or the creatures of this earth or even the fish of the sea ever, for one moment, look at you with concern?

Don't flatter yourself!

In all that God has created, it is only Christ who is concerned about "it," His imputed truth to you (1 Corinthians 7:21 ESV). Therefore, He gave His only Son to die for your sins, then sent His Spirit to teach you how to live!

Getting back to all that God created, we all would do well to let what the Lord made rest, for in doing this, our endless toil will cease, and we may spend our time reading His Word.

What if, for just a day, the believers' thoughts—their words—to one another were "Do not be concerned about it" (1 Corinthians 7:21)? Then believers went about their day, thinking of how many hours they may spend reading His Word instead of seeking to further their control over what God already gave them dominion of, as the Lord said at the end of the sixth day of creation:

> And God saw everything that He made, and behold, it was very good. And there was evening and there was morning, the sixth day. Genesis 1:28

As one who spent far too many years seeking to gain what is of no eternal value, God will spare us of that if we would only read what pertains to eternal life (1 Corinthians 7:28 ESV).

Trust that not for a second were Christ's interest ever divided (1 Corinthians 7:34 ESV). How far are we from being concerned with purity? Is there any who are actually anxious about the things of the Lord (1 Corinthians 7:34 ESV)?

Whose intent each day is to please their creator?

Who among us asks the Lord, "Teach me how to be holy in body and in spirit this day" (1 Corinthians 7:34 ESV)? It is Christ who has secured our salvation, so we live in devotion to what He commands (1 Corinthians 7:35 ESV).

Throughout your day, if you conclude that you have the Spirit of God, by all means, remain as a bond servant to Christ (1 Corinthians 7:22, 23, 36–40 ESV).

IT'S WHERE OUR WORDS COME FROM!

We ask of You, Lord, that You would apply Your Word in our life this day. In receiving Your truth, teach us how to find contentment in Your ways. May the concern of our lives be of becoming like Christ. Help us to want to spend ourselves devoted to what You have first given us—this imputed truth—in the form of letters on a page. Yet with Your Spirit, these words in Your scrolls are words of life!

Chapter 12

Exhort Others

Command and teach these things. Let no one despise you for your youth but set the believers as an example in your speech, in how you conduct yourself—may it be out of obedience in love, in faith, in purity to my Word.
—1 Timothy 4:11

"Devote yourselves to the public reading of My exhortations and teachings," says the Lord (1 Timothy 4:13 ESV).

In what we do, may our actions be proclaimed among others so that not us but Christ is manifested in our speech (1 Timothy 3:16 ESV). "Great indeed, we confess, is the mystery of godliness" (1 Timothy 3:16 ESV). Let all we do, Lord, be done so what is proclaimed, what is believed from us is that we are created in your image.

May it never be said of us, "O foolish and faithless," for our eyes read the words of those who saw that "Jesus Christ was publicly portrayed as crucified" (Galatians 3:1 ESV).

Let us be so bold to ask one another: Did you receive the Spirit of Christ (Galatians 3:2 ESV)? If you did receive Jesus Christ into your life, was it not then by faith and not by any work of your own (Galatians 3:2, ESV)? What you indeed received began not from human effort, rather from the spirit of the words of the author of life

(Galatians 3:3 ESV). Since Christ suffered once for the penalty of death for all, no longer allow yourselves to be constrained with sin; instead, live set free by the power of Christ. In believing in God, in Christ, you will be found as righteous (Galatians 3:5 ESV).

To give us a human example, help us, Lord, to live not glorifying what man made; instead, set Your promise that we were made in the likeness of Christ by the Spirit as the promise to believers (Galatians 3:15–18 ESV).

> Let no one disqualify you (Colossians 2:18).

> But share in suffering for the gospel by the power of God (2 Timothy 1:8).

As a tree planted by the water never goes dry, believers are to literally stand upon holy ground and stand among other believers so that the words from God being taught will bring life into their souls (Luke 6:43–49 ESV). Whether rich or poor, all believers need fellowship with one another (1 John 3:17 ESV). God knowing everything reassures His Word within us as we gather to promote His Word as truth (1 John 3:19–20 ESV).

God's love abides in Him, and where two or more are gathered together in His name to study His Word, then He, Christ, is among them (1 John 3:17–18 ESV). The value of your earthly condition, of your spiritual fellowship, all pertain to who Christ is. Our earthly riches have nothing to do with experiencing Christ (1 John 3:16–17 ESV). If we love God, one way to express His unmerited favor toward us is to set aside time with others for His kingdom's sake.

Releasing the word that is within us is in acts of obedience, for when our hearts condemn us to interact with other believers, the Spirit of God then has dominion among us to teach us truth (1 John 3:20 ESV).

Know that meeting together to study His Word pleases God (1 John 3:22 ESV).

Sure, Christ could have only preached to the multitudes (Matthew 5:1 ESV). Yet He chose disciples within whom to devote to the teachings of the kingdom of heaven, who were led by the Holy Spirit (Matthew 4:17, 19, 21, 23; Acts 6:2–4, ESV).

This is the commandment

> That we believe in the name of His Son Jesus Christ and love one another, just as He has commanded us (1 John 3:23).

This we know, Lord, that as we join together in abiding in Your Word, as we are led by Your Spirit, this Spirit, whom we have received in faith, will illuminate our hearts with Your truth (1 John 3:24).

Chapter 13

RANSOMED TO LIFE

*If it were not for Christ, we all would be
eternally found as traitors, imprisoned,
and condemned before a Holy God.*
—Isaiah 33:1

The previous things told to us by the Spirit remain true to us this day—that those who oppose Christ will be handed over to Satan for the destruction of their pride (Acts 1:1; 1 Timothy 1:20 ESV). While for us who believe the spirit of truth that confirms within us Christ's resurrection, we live both now, and eternally for the kingdom of God is given to us by Christ (Acts 1:1 ESV).

Listen to the instructions from those whom Christ has appointed over your soul, such as this command from Paul who spoke not of His own authority but of His Savior's (1 Timothy 1:1, 3 ESV). For those whom Christ entrusts as stewards of His church must be devoted to Christ (1 Timothy 1:4 ESV). Christ, who told His disciples to wait until they received the promise of the Holy Spirit given from the Father, is again commanded in the apostle Paul's words to remain for the purpose of edifying certain people (Acts 1:4; 1 Timothy 1:3–4 ESV).

Knowing that You are above our ways of understanding, "O Lord, be gracious to us; we wait for you" (Isaiah 33:2 ESV). Our waiting is not of inaction but of your divine purpose to be worked into us. Your stability secures us in times of troubles; Christ is our source of wisdom from our all-knowing creator (Isaiah 33:6 ESV).

Now concerning our sin, it was Christ who has offered Himself for "all of us" (1 Corinthians 8:1 ESV). Therefore, remind us as we ask in this "knowledge" of being forgiven to give compassion to others (1 Corinthians 8:1 ESV).

Take heart: this moment for Christ is concerned about us, for we are included with the one to whom said,

> You follow me! John 21:22

What Christ longs for everyone to grasp within their beings is John's profession of faith: "It is the Lord" (John 21:7 ESV)! In addition, what holds true for us is that Christ has authority over our lives, for He said, "If it is my will that he remain until I come" (John 21:23 ESV). Implying be concerned about your own salvation, if we remain on this earth or not is determined by God. If His Word remains within our souls is up to Christ. If believers are accepted into eternity remains to be decided (John 21:23 ESV).

Then if our lives belong to Christ, we are to live surrendered to whom God has predestined to join Him for eternity (John 21:23 ESV). So, believer, Jesus said before and says now, "What is that to you?" What concern is it to you who is forgiven and who is condemned? You spend yourselves on remaining as my disciples (John 21:23 ESV).

Possessing this attained wisdom from the Father—Christ builds us up in truth (1 Corinthians 8:1 ESV). In all of this seeking after godliness, what remains is it is the LORD who gives wisdom (1 Corinthians 8:2; Proverbs 2:6 ESV). For what we know is given to us and still we know, not as we ought to know, for if we were truly obedient, we would not sin against Christ (1 Corinthians 8:2 ESV).

What then is commended to us by grace is to know there are no gods while there is but one God (1 Corinthians 8:4–8 ESV). We are told, "There is no God but one" (1 Corinthians 8:4 ESV)!

IT'S WHERE OUR WORDS COME FROM!

How important is it that we search what has been foretold from long ago as many before us and among us today spend their lives living for, seeking after gods that are not real (1 Corinthians 8:4 ESV)? On earth and even into the heavens, some claim that so-called gods rule, yet, for us, there is one God, the Father of creation (1 Corinthians 8:5–6 ESV).

The Holy Spirit then testifies within our minds that though this remains true for us, not all people possess this knowledge of creation (1 Corinthians 8:7 ESV). Scripture tells us that the worship of false gods, idols, and even man-made items will not commend us with Christ (1 Corinthians 8:8 ESV). What remains is that not all should desire to teach the Word of God, for it is better for some to never hear the Gospel than to have their ears receive false doctrine (1 Corinthians 8:8 ESV). Take care then on how you present yourselves as workmen who can rightly divide the gospel message of Jesus Christ, through whom all things exist (1 Corinthians 8:6, 9 ESV).

If you say that you are a Christian, yet others see you acting in disobedience to the commands of Christ, how will your conduct lead others into repentance (1 Corinthians 8:10 ESV)? Not some but all gain strength from purity (1 Corinthians 8:10–13 ESV).

Our instructions from God

In faith of Christ, put an end to your former habits of sin as Christ died to entrust to you His Gospel (1 Corinthians 8:11 ESV).

> The fear of the LORD is the beginning of knowledge; fools despise wisdom and instruction (Proverbs 1:7).

Chapter 14

Impartial

Father of lights, distribute Your Word among us equally (Acts 6:1 ESV). For in doing this, You prove again to us that You show no partiality or favoritism, as we, those who belong to Christ, are the same (Acts 10:34 ESV).

Restore us to Yourself, O Lord, that we may be restored (Lamentations 5:21 ESV). Renew our days as of old unless You have decided to utterly reject us forever. We implore of You, our creator and sustainer of life, to remember that we are mere dust (Lamentations 5:21–22; Genesis 2:7 ESV).

If we believe that You, our Christ, are of the descendants of David, the king, then why do we doubt that You, Lord, were raised of the likeness of mankind such as Adam (Genesis 2:7 ESV)? To then be lifted up upon Your cross, only to behold the shame and the disgrace of the world as it was You, Christ, who were despised and rejected by men (Isaiah 53:2–3 ESV).

To this day, Father it, is Christ as the One to whom we hide our faces, for He alone is pure (Isaiah 53:3 ESV). How blind we are, Lord, in calling You the traitor when it is us who have betrayed you (Isaiah 33:1 ESV).

Ready us then with your outstretched arms once more, not that you would be crucified a second time rather that, every morning in faith, we could receive grace upon grace into our souls (Isaiah 33:2 ESV).

Lord, give us courage to stand firm upon the rock of Calvary, for when others fled from Your cross, may we remain (Isaiah 33:3 ESV). In truth, Lord, Your Spirit was set above Jerusalem as You ascended unto the Father (Isaiah 33:5 ESV).

Our Lord, Savior and King of the Jews, we believe with justice and righteousness that you have given stability in our present times to abound for Zion's treasure that has been released into our souls (Isaiah 33:5–6 ESV).

Our imputed truth is in Your words as You declared:

> "Now I will arise," says the Lord,
> now I will lift myself up;
> now I will be exalted." Isaiah 33:10

We give back Your Word unto you, God, for You, our Lord, are our judge, our advocate. As the law of creation belongs to You, as our God, you live in unapproachable light; truly You are our salvation (Isaiah 33:22 ESV).

Hear Your Word spoken, for our confidence is that we also belong of the descendants of Adam; our souls have returned unto You out of doubt into faith. Once again, Lord, look upon us that we who are of Christ may be pleasant in Your sight (Genesis 2:8–9 ESV).

Any good in us is of Christ, the good treasure, that has broken free from the grave and into our hearts (Luke 6:45; Isaiah 33:6 ESV). Only You, our Messiah, would praise the Father in Your betrayal, as You, Lord, knew soon all things would be made new (John 13:26–32, 19:25–27, 30 ESV).

How is it, Lord, that you foreknew that Your garments would be divided, and yet You endured the cross for us (John 19:24 ESV)? Our Lord and our God, we are unworthy to read Your words to Your mother, for as You were bound and nailed to Your cross, You said,

> "Woman, behold, your Son." John 19:25–26

To this day, it is us who need You, Lord. Take hold of our lives how You so please to do so. In Your name, all these things have occurred. Amen.

Jesus prays for us

> O righteous Father, even though the world does not know you, I know you, and these know that you have sent me. I made known to them your name, and I will continue to make it known, that the love with which you have loved me may be in them, and I in them. John 17:25–26

Chapter 15

Share Jesus

"Certain persons, by swerving from these, have wandered away into vain discussion" (1 Timothy 1:6).

In "desiring to be teachers of the law, without understanding either what they are saying or the things about which they make confident assertation," people can be mistaught (1 Timothy 1:7).

Our hope as believers who seek to become true in the faith of Christ Jesus our Lord is to be discipled by grace, mercy, and peace from the Father (1 Timothy 1:12 ESV).

As believers, our hope is to attain that Jesus Christ might display His perfect patience to others from our conduct (1 Timothy 1:16 ESV).

For the ungodly, the discipline of the Lord will teach them not to profane His name (1 Timothy 1:20 ESV). For those dignified by the gospel of Christ, persist in supplications, prayers, intercessions, and thanksgivings that are given by God for believers and for all people (1 Timothy 2:1–2 ESV). The plan of God is to give us of Himself as we set our faith in Him, God commands we then live a quiet peaceful godly life as bestowed from God to true believers (1 Timothy 1:2, 2:2 ESV). Faith in Christ brings joy to the Father (1 Timothy 2:3–4).

Sharing the message of Christ with believers and not-yet believers brings joy to our Creator who has made us capable to speak

His Word as we are gathered together (1 Timothy 2:3–4 ESV). For everyone who desires God, all people who profess Christ as Lord and Savior, find peace in the sight of their creator (1 Timothy 2:3–4 ESV).

Even further than saying "God is God" is knowing what pleases the Lord is not only for His name to be exalted, yet what our creator finds pleasure in is when we, whom He has created, finally takes hold of His Word for what it truly is—the knowledge of truth (1 Timothy 2:4 ESV).

God's Word tells us that the gospel we are to share with other's says, "For there is one God, and there is one mediator between God and men, the man Christ Jesus, who gave himself as a ransom for all, which is the testimony given at the proper time" (1 Timothy 2:5–6 ESV).

Christ is the Son of God. As one with God, Christ was the only one who could satisfy the Lord's demands for our condemned souls. So with the only appointed person to fulfill what was written before His birth, God sent Christ to bring us into the foreknowledge founded upon Jesus and His teachings to us.

The verses you have read from the Bible were written from a man who was shown mercy and grace by God as He, too, at one time blasphemed the God who created him (1 Timothy 1:20, 2:7; Acts 9:1–9 ESV).

What are believers to do with their life? "Seek and read from the book of the Lord" (Isaiah 34:16 ESV).

Look for others who know the Word of God to teach you, and then Christ will give you the knowledge of truth (Acts 9:11 ESV). Then remember, once you receive Christ, never forget who you were without this knowledge of forgiveness. Remind yourself that God in Christ forgave you while you cursed Him.

> Rise and go to the street called Straight, and at the house of Judas look for a man of Tarsus named Saul, for behold, he is praying. Acts 9:11

IT'S WHERE OUR WORDS COME FROM!

What is the path that leads to life called? The path is a highway called the way of holiness. Whose feet takes hold of this highway? *It*. This path belongs only to those who are permitted to walk on the way (Isaiah 35:8 ESV).

> For the unclean shall not pass over it.
> Isaiah 35:8

Nor any ravenous beast is allowed upon it, for they shall not be found there (Isaiah 25:9 ESV). While the redeemed of the LORD shall return to the LORD by His Word (Isaiah 35:9 ESV).

Those of God being the ransomed of Christ may enter fellowship with God by believing in Christ (Isaiah 35:10 ESV). The New Jerusalem is full of praises and singing with everlasting joy obtained and kept for believers on the highway to life (Isaiah 35:10 ESV).

The obstacles are gone. Christ supernaturally brings His people home, who have been conditioned in a life of obedience and purity (1 Corinthians 9:12 ESV). Believers are now fit to endure anything as nothing is in the way of the gospel of Christ.

Therefore, live for Christ

> Preach the Word; be ready in
> season and out of season;
> reprove, rebuke, and exhort, with
> complete patience and teaching.
> 2 Timothy 4:2

Remain on the highway of life, for some will wander off accumulating nonsense or false doctrines to suit their own passions (2 Timothy 4:4 ESV). While for us who believe, always be sober-minded, endure suffering, do the work of an evangelist, and fulfill your ministry entrusted to you by Christ (2 Timothy 4:5 ESV).

Stay on the highway of life as a drink offering that is poured out first by Christ then from yourself for the sake of others for whom Christ died (2 Timothy 4:6 ESV). The prize of the kingdom of heaven is in heaven, so by all means, finish the race, saying to one another and to Christ, I, since Christ enabled me to, "I have kept the faith" (2 Timothy 4:7 ESV). Again, Lord, we respond to Your invitation as of those who love you are appearing to us on Your behalf, for apart from You, we can do nothing (2 Timothy 4:8; Acts 9:3 ESV).

Chapter 16

FOLLOWING AFTER

We love because He first loved us.
—1 John 4:19

And this is the testimony—that God gave us eternal life and this life is in His Son. Whoever has the Son has life; whoever does not have the Son of God does not have life (1 John 5:11–12 ESV). And we know that the Son of God has come and has given us understanding so that we may know Him who is true, and we are in Him who is true, in His Son, Jesus Christ (1 John 5:20 ESV).

He is the true God and eternal life.
1 John 5:20

How did we get this promise of everlasting life?

Since we could not keep the perfect law of God, only from His Word may we receive the promise of salvation.

Lord, may we receive the promise of salvation from His Word, from Christ's words as He is the author of life. Christ is the perfector of life in whom we trust. Help us this day, Lord, to believe.

Word upon word, precept of precept, angel after angel, believer by believer imply all things belong to God (Galatians 3:18–20 ESV).

And yet still what was needed was for Christ to remain as our intermediary between the Father and us (Galatians 3:20 ESV). Even sin is bound and imprisoned under Christ's authority. We believe in the One who is able to give us this eternal promise of life (Galatians 3:21–22 ESV). By keeping the law of God, Christ has dominion of everything, including us (Galatians 3:21-22, ESV).

In the book of Genesis

"The LORD God took the man and put him [Adam] in the garden of Eden to work it," to maintain "it," and to keep it (Genesis 2:15 ESV).

In all of this reading of God wanting to make us able to know and understand His Word—if and it's a big *if*—if understanding of the knowledge of good and evil were in the tree of life, why then was man restricted from eating the fruit of the tree (Genesis 2: 17 ESV)?

Have you not read and heard that salvation belongs to Christ alone?

Limitations on our freedom are meant for our good. God knowing each soul must choose Him willingly—provided us with His Word, His Son, His Spirit, and His divine Word remains that we may receive God (Luke 6:43–45 ESV).

Adam and Eve were told not to eat of the tree, for God commanded not to eat of it. In God's design, He, God, was with Adam and Eve, concluding what further knowledge could they possible receive from eating of a tree (Genesis 2:5–8 ESV)?

Their choice was doubting that God's presence with them in the garden wasn't sufficient, for within their sinful nature apart from constant fellowship with the Father, sin occurred.

Now for us, after Christ's life, death, and resurrection, this constant fellowship with God belongs to the Helper, the Holy Spirit that was sent to us from God (Luke 24:44–49 ESV).

We may now eat and do as we so choose, for Christ now lives in us—if and it's a personal *if*—if we profess Christ as Lord of our life.

Before Christ's birth, we are told by our Creator who has formed us: "Fear not, for I," Your Creator, have redeemed you, and you will be called Christians by my name. For you are mine, says the Lord (Isaiah 43:1 ESV).

The resurrected Christ is the fruit of life

Jesus told His disciples, "Everything written before and after me is from God" (Luke 24:44 ESV). Then the promise, far better than the fruit of the garden, was given to the disciples as Jesus opened their minds to understand Scripture (Luke 24:45 ESV).

What then began in the garden ended with Christ as in His suffering, we who believe are forgiven and made new from within (Luke 24:47 ESV).

Our God, our Maker and Giver of life, in your Spirit, guide us. For You have made Your Word accessible to and within us. What remains is for You to lead us. Since You live in us, we ask that You guide what we do and say from Your written Word, then empower Your Word in our minds by Your Spirit. We ask this in Christ's name. Amen and amen.

Chapter 17

CREATION

*God saw everything that He had made,
and behold, it was very good.*
—Genesis 1:31

Very soon in creation, God would make a helper fit for Adam (Genesis 2:18 ESV). God, knowing it was not good for man to be alone, went far beyond, surrounding us with other believers, for the Lord our God sent His own Spirit to abide within the facets of our minds (Genesis 2:18 ESV).

On what do you rest this trust of yours? Isaiah 36:4

It is implied that Adam and Eve were not to set their trust upon each other; instead; God and His given commands were to determine their actions and choices. As the Lord God said,

What is this that you have done? Genesis 3:13

Did I not command you not to eat of the tree in the midst of the garden (Genesis 2:17 ESV)?

IT'S WHERE OUR WORDS COME FROM!

After going against the Word from the Lord, do you think that mere words of blaming one another will wash away your sin (Isaiah 36:5 ESV)? For Eve blamed the serpent, telling God, "The serpent deceived me, and I ate" (Genesis 3:13 ESV). And Adam said, "The woman whom you gave to be with me, she gave me fruit of the tree, and I ate" (Genesis 3:12 ESV).

"In whom do you now trust, that you have rebelled against me?" said the Lord (Isaiah 36:5 ESV). Such as Adam and Eve, God will ask you one day, "What have you done?"

The gospel of what Jesus began to do and is doing still is this: **Jesus finds joy in living for God**.

For God anointed Jesus of Nazareth with the Holy Spirit and with power. How then Jesus went about doing good and healing all who were oppressed by the devil was because God was with him (Acts 10:38 ESV).

Christ was put to death by being hung on a tree (Acts 10:39 ESV). But God, to whom Christ is obedient, raised Jesus on the third day and made Jesus appear in His resurrected body (Acts 10:40 ESV).

Jesus in His glorified body was only known by His disciples for such as not all will believe in Christ. Neither will those who disbelieve be witnessed to forever (Acts 10:41 ESV).

Take it one way or the other

The Gospel is offered to you for a certain time. The days of God offering Christ to you, one day, will cease.

In His final eternal condition, Christ commanded the first disciples to preach what you have just read to others. The power of the cross is that Jesus is the One appointed by God to oversee all of humanity (Acts 10:42 ESV). Even more, Christ became the judge of those who have lived and of the living (Acts 10:42 ESV).

For any who seek Christ, for you who want to confess the Lord Jesus as your Savior, the gospel is this: Everyone who believes in Him now receives forgiveness of sins through His name that was nailed above His cross (Acts 10:4; John 19:19 ESV).

One day, everything about your life will be measured by God in evaluation of what you believe of Christ. For it was written on His tree that He bore for your sins. In words or in your mind, you believe one or the other:

> Jesus of Nazareth, the King of the Jews.
> John 19:19

Others will say,

> Do not write, "The King of the Jews," but rather, "This man said, 'I am King of the Jews.'"
> John 19:21

As such, the LORD's Word is final. Pilate said, "What I have written I have written," (John 19:22 ESV).
What then do you believe of Christ?
One day, the Father will say either of the two words to each of us: "Enter and receive the joy from My salvation given to you" or "Depart from me, for I never knew you."
Let us live anticipating eternal words from our Creator that is keeping track of all He is doing in our lives. For the gospel is this: Salvation belongs to Christ alone.
God has made faith in Christ possible as some belong to Him:

> For you are a people holy to the
> LORD your God. The LORD your God
> has chosen you to be a people for
> His treasured possession, out of all
> the peoples who are on the face of
> the earth. (Deuteronomy 7:6 ESV)

God is long suffering that He seeks for everyone to repent and receive Christ.

IT'S WHERE OUR WORDS COME FROM!

Will you receive the gospel of Christ today by confessing to God:

> Lord, I'm a sinner, and I'm living for God now.
> I need Jesus to free me of all my past and future sins.
> I want to spend eternity worshiping God with my family and friends who are believers, and for those who are yet to believe, transform their hearts as well.
> I choose to believe in Jesus Christ as my Lord and my Savior on this day. Jesus, I accept you as my one and only God.
> For believing in Jesus is accepting the gospel, I, Lord, accept the message of Christ.
> I believe Christ defeated death and rose from His grave.
> I invite the living Christ to live in my soul beginning now.
> In Jesus's name. Amen.

Jesus told His disciples in a matter of words to live in reverence of God, while at the same time, living in the truth that all our sins were judged by God at Jesus's cross, we stand forgiven by Jesus's blood, purity, and in His righteousness.

The best part is that those sins of ours are forgotten by God; He remembers them no more (Hebrews 10:17 ESV).

Christ has imputed His truth to us as His Gospel is complete, for where there is forgiveness of these sins of ours, there no longer is a requirement to pay the penalty of sin (Hebrews 10:18 ESV). The spirit of truth has been given to us as the law of the Lord is in our hearts, then as we read His Word, *it* is being written in our minds (Hebrews 10:16 ESV).

Christ makes it possible for the Holy Spirit to bring to remembrance all that Christ began to do and teach, beginning with reading

His Word. As Jesus said, "I am with you always to the end of the age." This is another of Christ's references that, in His ascension, the Holy Spirit will descend from heaven to remain with believers (Matthew 28:20 ESV).

So then speak truth with one another, for faith comes by hearing the Word of the Lord (the Holy Bible ESV).

> Today, if you hear His voice,
> do not harden your hearts.
> Hebrews 4:7 ESV

For you, new believer, who have recommitted your soul to Christ this day, may you search and find what was written long ago:

> For He has somewhere spoken of the seventh day in this way: And God rested on the seventh day from all His works. Hebrews 4:4

Christ tells us rest is given to us who believe that all things have been made by God for you. Your salvation is kept in heaven by Christ who has made you well this day!

Believer, may this be said of your new life in Christ as you begin to recount all that the LORD our God has done for you, and may others say this as well: "And what more shall I say? For time would fail me to tell" of all that Christ began in my life (Hebrews 11:32 ESV).

Chapter 18

From Him

*In your struggle against sin you have not yet
resisted to the point of shedding your blood.*
—Hebrews 12:4

Keep yourself pure and from being undone by deceit (Hebrews 12:15 ESV).

> See to it that no one fails to obtain the grace of God; that no "root of bitterness" springs up and causes trouble, and by it many become defiled (Hebrews 12:15 ESV).

Examine the Word of the Lord yourself to discover that your freedom to share the gospel belongs in Christ (1 Corinthians 9:1–3, 16 ESV).

Such as Christ entrusted His apostleship to Paul, believers base their faith upon Christ' works; not man's nor the words of nonbelievers (1 Corinthians 9:1–2 ESV). The life you now live is being transformed by the message of Jesus' life. His promise to remake us stands for what we are becoming is from our Lord (1 Corinthians 9:2 ESV).

In all ways boast of how the Spirit of the Lord, is transforming your life, how the power of the resurrected Christ is reforming you by

His Word. Share how word-by-word Christ's workmanship of re-creating you into His likeness is on display in your life (1 Corinthians 9:1–2 ESV). By all means, boast the ways of the Spirit of the Lord, how the power of the resurrected Christ is showing you word by word that we are His workmanship created to thrive in the likeness of our Creator who is being revealed to us (1 Corinthians 9:1–2 ESV). For from glory to glory, Christ seals our souls with forgiveness (1 Corinthians 9:2 ESV).

It is written about Jesus our Lord, who has sealed our discipleship (1 Corinthians 9:2 ESV). Know, therefore, your calling as a disciple of Christ is not meant to constrain you, or to hinder you, rather what we receive and know as truth from Scripture is to allow us to expound upon what has been written (1 Corinthians 9:3–7 ESV). So, we are not to spend our days criticizing other believers, instead we are to live at peace encouraged by the Spirit of grace that was offered to us by Christ. We are to serve God and one another without complaint, for the Lord loves a cheerful disciple (1 Corinthians 9:3–7, 10:10 ESV).

> So, whether you eat or drink, or whatever you do, do all to the glory of God.
> 1 Corinthians 10:31

Live with a clear conscience, making the best use of each day (1 Corinthians 10:24 ESV). Live enjoying what the Lord has first given to each of us, "for the earth is the Lord's and the fullness thereof" (1 Corinthians 10:26 ESV). The authority of Scripture, the authority of Christ is offered to you as well; this imperishable salvation then belongs to each person who participates in surrendering their souls to Christ (Corinthians 9:8, 25 ESV).

However, each of us is earning our living is of little concern, for what is of eternal importance is that when we gather, we gather in the name of Christ, sharing the bounty of our efforts in seeking after what pertains to our spiritual lives (1 Corinthians 9:6–12 ESV).

The expense of becoming a disciple of Christ was paid by none of us as our Savior gave His life of His own accord (1 Corinthians 9:7 ESV).

Again, make use of the day while the concern of our God is to disciple you into the likeness of Christ (1 Corinthians 9:12 ESV). What we learn in Scripture is that we have this freedom in Christ to be disciples no matter our title or occupation. For none are useless; rather, all are joint heirs with Christ. Live confident that any obstacle put before you, our Lord has already defeated and overcome. Disciples believe nothing can get in the way of the gospel of Jesus Christ (1 Corinthians 9:12 ESV).

Lord of creation, with grateful souls, we rejoice that we get to inherit the kingdom of heaven both in eternity and now living by the gospel of Christ (1 Corinthians 9:14 ESV).

Chapter 19

One God

*Little children, you are from God and
have overcome them, for he who is in you
is greater than he who is in the world.*
—1 John 4:4

Therefore, may you have this confidence to proclaim not to some but to all whose hearts have become proud. "The Word of the Lord came to me," and God has this against you (Ezekiel 28:1–2 ESV).

"Because your heart is proud," and you claim yourself above God (Ezekiel 28:2 ESV). "And yet you are but the offspring of sin inherited from Adam," thus says the Lord to you (Ezekiel 28:1 ESV). "You are no god. Wait and see as I," says the Lord, "will bring the most ruthless of the nations against you" (Ezekiel 28:2, 7 ESV). In time you will be thrust down to the bottomless pit, and then will you still say, 'I am a god' (Ezekiel 28:8–9)? Before foreigners surround you to destroy you, draw near to Me while you still can," declares the Lord (Ezekiel 28:7, 10 ESV).

And now, Lord, before we say anymore lest our hearts grow proud, remind us we are nothing without Your Word! For what would we say without Your divine truth? Lest we speak in error, allow Your Holy Spirit to teach us what Your Word says. As Scripture confirms itself, may what we say be true. Show us the good in Your Word. amen.

Moreover, as the same word came to Ezekiel the priest, as the hand of the Lord was upon him prior—now from prince to king—the Lord says, "You were the signet of perfection, full of wisdom and perfect in beauty. You were in Eden, the garden of God; every precious stone was your covering, until" (Ezekiel 1:3, 28:11–13 ESV).

"On the day that you were created, *it* was I," says the Lord, "who anointed you as a guardian cherub. As you were on my holy mountain, you walked where few ever have" (Ezekiel 28:13–14 ESV).

"Until unrighteousness was found in you, you were blameless in your ways" (Ezekiel 28:15 ESV).

Lest our hearts become proud, may we this day not even set our words against the evil one; rather let us say, "The Lord rebuke you, O evil one" (the Holy Bible ESV).

For your heart grew dim as you were filled with violence, and you sinned (Ezekiel 28:16 ESV).

"So I cast you as a profane thing from the mountain of God, and I destroyed you, O guardian cherub" that you once were (Ezekiel 28:16 ESV).

From the heart of the stones of fire being the presence of glory, the love of the Lord departed from you now, O evil one (Ezekiel 28:16–17 ESV). The praise of others became your fault, for the pride of my perfection in making you corrupted your soul (Ezekiel 28:17 ESV).

"Therefore, the stones of fire of my purity," says the Lord, "is the consuming fire from my righteous indignation against you. Now, all, even I, are appalled at you (Ezekiel 28:16–19 ESV).

From my sight, all who saw you labeled you as forsaken as you are called into my sanctuary nevermore (Ezekiel 28:18–19 ESV).

Therefore, since our hearts can lead us into condemnation, such has become of Lucifer, do what you must Lord to keep our hearts surrendered to you God (1 John 3:19–24 ESV).

Chapter 20

Faith

But say the word, and let my servant be healed.
—Luke 7:7

Faith of Christ is offered to everyone fairly as *it* says the path of righteousness is level, for our God still, to this day, makes it possible for all to believe in Him (Isaiah 26:7 ESV).

The battle for your soul will be tested. Will you allow persuasive words to entertain your minds or will you listen to truth confirming the messengers of the Lord as "we trust in the Lord our God" (Isaiah 36:7 ESV)?

The attack against your faith in God is what the evil one has sought to conquer from creation unto this current day (Isaiah 36:1–2; Genesis 2:10–15 ESV). The devil seeks to divide God, the source of life, from His believers.

The battle for the Word of God to be taught is between truth and lies. As the power of our creator took Adam and set him in the garden of Eden. God sought for Adam to yes, tend to the garden while the emphasis was for Adam to care for Eve (Genesis 2:15–16 ESV).

Now we are told that the king of Assyria was going against all the fortified cities of Judah, being the creator's people (Isaiah 36:1 ESV). The constant of life is that for infants, such as Adam in a world

IT'S WHERE OUR WORDS COME FROM!

by himself, or for the elderly confined by the limitations of a body, each must be led by others (John 21:18 ESV).

Jesus spoke to His disciples, saying:

> Truly, truly, I say to you, when you were young, you used to dress yourself and walk wherever you wanted, but when you are old, you will stretch out your hands, and another will dress you and carry you where you do not want to go. John 21:18

Now there are also many other things that Jesus did. Were every one of them to be written, I suppose that the world itself could not contain the books that would be written (John 21:25 ESV).

How do we get from being infants who are dependent on others to becoming like the infinite? The way is by faith in Christ!

What then determines a person's life is their personal faith in God. The Bible records the life of one infant who was set in a basket then led away from any comfort from others, for it was Moses who was in the currents of the Nile on his own (Isaiah 36:3; Exodus 1:22, 2:1–4 ESV).

What drives the minds of evil? Fear is how evil causes us to first doubt God, then followed by the lie of the wicked one. In the insecurity of God, evil seeks to eliminate God's Word and those who speak God's Word (Exodus 1:8–10 ESV).

What was said by foreign men of faith who opposed the creator? "Come, let us deal shrewdly with them, lest they multiply, and, if war breaks out, they join our enemies and fight against us and escape from the land" (Exodus 1:10).

What God is offering to you this day is grace, yet you have to receive it. God's divine forbearance to spare the life of Moses was in that, as an infant, as a three-month-old baby, others rescued him (Exodus 2:2, 5 ESV).

We are told that women went to the river, and one woman, seeing this basket, knelt down and took the basket from the reeds (Exodus 2:5 ESV). When she opened it, she saw the child and took pity on him (Exodus 2:5–6 ESV). This servant woman who discovered Moses reminds us God looks at us with compassion (Matthew 5:12 ESV).

Such as the Word of God, what was within this basket was unknown to the women—that is, until she opened it (Exodus 2:6–9 ESV). We must read to gain faith. Christ's imputed truth to us is said that He, Jesus, opened the scroll and began to teach from it (Luke 4:16–21 ESV).

And the scroll of the prophet Isaiah was given to Him, to Jesus. He unrolled the scroll and found the place where it was written, and He, Jesus, rolled up the scroll and gave it back to the attendant and sat down (Luke 4:17, 20 ESV).

What did Jesus say that caused all to marvel? Jesus had said this as He taught:

> The Spirit of the Lord is upon me, because He [the Father] has anointed me to proclaim good news to the poor. He has sent me to proclaim liberty to the captives and recovering of sight to the blind, to set at liberty those who are oppressed, to proclaim the year of the Lord's favor. Luke 4:18–19

What was given to the woman was the ability to nurse Moses, then earn her rightful wages (Exodus 2:9 ESV). The same holds true for men who can rightly divide the word of truth for since the birth of Christ's church, those who teach should earn their living teaching the truth of Scripture (1 Corinthians 9:14 ESV).

The illustration tells us not to hinder an ox as it treads out grain (1 Corinthians 9:8–12 ESV). We must then share what is written with others!

The spiritual battle

In defiance against our creator, the accusation is the Word against the world. So, God, help us this day to remain faithful and obedient to what is written of Christ!

Chapter 21

ALL BELONGS

Recount then how all of this within
His Word is the LORD*'s doing.*
—Acts 7:30–34

From the beginning there has been the battle against persuasive speech (Isaiah 36:8 ESV).

> Come now, make a wager with my master.
> (Isaiah 36:8 ESV)

Could these words be even slyer than the devil's words to Christ…"if you are the Son of God, then…" (Matthew 4:3, 6 ESV).

Next the devil said to Jesus, "All these I will give you, if you will fall down and worship me" (Matthew 4:9 ESV).

Also, it was spoken: "Do not let Hezekiah deceive you, for he will not be able to deliver you" (Isaiah 36:14 ESV).

These forsaken words bring doubt into people's minds as "this is the spirit of the antichrist" (1 John 4:3 ESV). Know that the Antichrist has been in the world since the beginning (1 John 4:3; Genesis 3:1; Isaiah 36:8 ESV).

Words from the Antichrist are the following:

> But if you say to me, "We trust in the LORD our God," is it not he whose high places and altars Hezikiah has removed? Isaiah 36:7

The lie that was planted prior follows:

> Come now, let us reason together (Isaiah 1:18 ESV).

> Turn now, every one of you, from his evil way and evil deeds, and dwell upon the land that the LORD has given to you and your fathers from of old and forever. Jeremiah 25:5

Moreover, if you hear the voice of the LORD, do not harden your hearts but receive what the church, His bride, has to say to you. Allow Christ to speak life into your soul (Jeremiah 25:10 ESV).

Persist to share with others what the LORD first gives you (Jeremiah 25:4 ESV). Do not provoke the LORD to anger with disobedient actions or muted ears; rather, listen and obey what you hear from your Maker (Jeremiah 25:6–7 ESV).

Submit to the LORD, for following after false teachings, idols, and foreign gods is harmful to you (Jeremiah 25:6–7 ESV).

Believers gain courage, for our accusers' conscience is weak (1 Corinthians 8:10 ESV). Pray that you grow in godliness lest you, too, disbelieve. Amen.

For if I preach the gospel, that gives me no ground for boasting. For necessity is laid upon me. Woe to me if I do not preach the gospel (1 Corinthians 9:16).

Believers boast of being known by the Gospel that lives within each soul, which is then constrained to share Christ's life, death, resurrection, and ascension with all who will listen (1 Corinthians 9:16 ESV).

IT'S WHERE OUR WORDS COME FROM!

The distinction of voices

Lord, we ask for discernment with who to believe and who to question and even proclaim as false witnesses of the Gospel. We ask that You teach us how to separate truth from the lie. What we know, as for those who confess, Jesus Christ as sent from heaven to us—this we believe. Then it is easy to acknowledge that those of the Antichrist who say Jesus is not of the Lord.

What then is ever conflicting is what we cannot see in the spiritual realm. Many people of the world speak what the people of the world want to hear. While we who belong to You, Lord, gather to hear of the One, Jesus Christ, who has overcome this world in His sinless life. "By this we know the Spirit of truth and the spirit of error" (1 John 4:1–6).

Know that all become like the voice you listen to. While none of us can avoid hearing others speak, how we react to the voices we hear is what then determines what we believe.

For the men of God in hearing Rabshakeh's pronouncement against the man Hezekiah, whom they knew and trusted, the men of God were silent and answered Rabshakeh not a word. For prior to this, they were told by King Hezekiah's command, "Do not answer him" (Isaiah 36:21 ESV).

So what will it be for you? Will you make your peace with God's accuser, then join in with a deceitful voice? Or will you remain faithful to the Holy Spirit who speaks within you, reminding you all that you have been taught from others of faith and from your Lord and Savior, Jesus the Christ—that Christ is the voice to respond to (Isaiah 36:16, 21).

The men of God who heard the lie tore their clothes in reaction to the disgrace against their Lord as believers were given to tear their clothes in outrage (Isaiah 36:22, 37:4 ESV).

In your life, there are those who go against the will of the Lord, for your own ears will hear what you do not want to hear. And yet God allows this.

Will you say this day is a day of distress, when rebuke is required? Isaiah 37:1–3

Some will be misled, even mocking their Creator, saying: "The LORD will deliver us" (Isaiah 36:18 ESV).

Isaiah's instructions

> Do it all for the sake of the gospel.
> 1 Corinthians 9:23

The law of Christ is for those who are under God's covenant of grace (1 Corinthians 9:19–21 ESV). Though Christ gave His life for any who would believe in Him, those under the law must obey (1 Corinthians 9:20 ESV). Believers are told to become familiar with other customs inviting them to take hold of the message of salvation while speaking truth to them yet remaining silent before false gods (Isaiah 36:21 ESV).

The commission from Christ to His disciples and for all of us is to go about teaching others to observe all that He, being Jesus, have told you (Matthew 28:20 ESV).

Chapter 22

Forever

Words from our Lord

> And behold, I am with you always, to the end of the age. Matthew 28:20

> Go into all the world and proclaim the gospel to the whole creation. Mark 16:15

Lest the Lord visits us and finds us in disbelief and rebukes us, we are to go about this day in faith that Christ is resurrected from the dead (Mark 16:14 ESV).

It is told in Scripture that the serpent is craftier than anything or anyone that the Lord has created, and yet he remains in this world seeking to divide believers from their creator (Genesis 3:1 ESV).

What is true for us, such as with Adam and Eve, is that God makes Himself known to us! He, God the Father, was heard walking in the garden in the cool of the day (Genesis 3:8 ESV). What Adam and Eve did is how far too many of us live; we react to God's invitation by deliberately blocking God out of our lives (Genesis 3:8 ESV).

Using something to hide themselves from their creator Adam and Eve hindered the working of the Holy Spirit (Genesis 3:8 ESV).

What we commonly know as trees is what Adam and Eve hid behind; what is keeping you from God?

And still unending in love, God asked them, "Where are you?" Genesis 3:9

Know that the Holy Spirit searches this earth longing for a soul to find rest in (the Holy Bible ESV).

While simultaneously the devil roams about seeking whom to destroy, while the battle for your souls goes on, you remain in Christ (the Holy Bible ESV).

Adam and Eve knew, as we know, when it is that God is calling us (Genesis 3:10 ESV).

Adam said, "I heard."

God was not pleased by Eve and Adam; God was not pleased, for many of whom were His chosen people who were overthrown by worry, doubt, and fear as they gave in to sin against the LORD (1 Corinthians 10:5 ESV). Help us, Lord, and strengthen us at once!

It—our Maker's imputed truth to us—holds true today in saying, "Now these things took place as examples for us that we might not desire evil as they did" (1 Corinthians 10:6 ESV).

The person with a disobedient soul never has eternal rest (Hebrews 3:17–18 ESV).

Asking then of our creator to awaken us in hearing His truth, lest we drift away from sound reasoning, we must pay attention to what is written and spoken of Christ (Hebrews 2:1 ESV).

As what was heard from angels has been found as reliable and trustworthy, so then how can anyone escape if this great salvation from Christ is neglected (Hebrews 2:2–3 ESV)? What was first spoken by our Lord, then attested to His disciples is that the Father confirms these things of Christ's life with many signs gifted to us by the Holy Spirit (Hebrews 2:3–4 ESV).

If you are yet to gain reverence for the Lord, this might help: when the unclean spirit has gone out of a person, it passes through waterless places seeking rest and finding none. It says, "I will return to my house (speaking of that person) from which I, being the demon, came." And when it (not imputed truth, rather a demonic spirit) comes, it (the devil) finds the house (a person) swept (with a sound mind) and put in order (functioning properly).

Then it (the wicked spirit) goes and brings seven other spirits more evil than itself, and they enter and dwell (in the soul of that person) there. And the last state of that person is worse than the first (Luke 11:24–26 ESV).

Lord, if we know anything, it is this that the Spirit of the Lord will not abide in man forever (Genesis 6:3 ESV)! Yet for us who believe one day, we will dwell in your kingdom forever.

Where the question of whom we spent our life serving is irrelevant, for our concern will be: "What God will you serve us this day as we sit and dine with our creator?" Joshua 24:15

And there was "one day," Lord, as written in the book that you have given us, this Holy Bible where we read that one of the men of renown faith—Joshua—asked you, Lord, to stop the sun and the moon so that your nation could defeat your enemies (Joshua 10:12–14 ESV).

For each of us, Lord, let us then ask in faith, the kind of faith where we ask what both pleases you and that we ask without doubting. Give us confidence to believe what is written in the contents of Christ's life. Amen.

And What Remains

Christ is the overcomer.

> For everyone who has been born of God overcomes the world. And this is the victory that has overcome the world—our faith.
> Who is it that overcomes the world except the one who believes that Jesus is the Son of God?
> 1 John 5:4–5

Chapter 23

Poured Out

It began in an instant—the origins of life.

> Living in the full assurance of this hope in Christ we persevere until the end. Hebrews 6:11

> And we say-oh, give thanks to the Lord, for He is good (Psalm 107:1 ESV).

When God makes a promise, telling us He will bless and keep us, we have already received and obtained what was previously unattainable for us (Hebrews 6:13–15 ESV). God, beyond our human understanding, made an oath to Abraham, including us within this oath. This oath is final; for Christ's life, death, and resurrection confirm the eternal promise that the Lord told Abraham—that He would multiply his descendants after him (Hebrews 6:13–16 ESV).

God put His oath into humanity with the life of His Son (Hebrews 6:13–20 ESV). To convince us of His promise, God guaranteed His Word with His life—the life of Christ (Hebrews 6:17 ESV). To bring His Word to life within Christ, it is both Jesus and the Word of God, both divine, that have human origins, as the character of the Word, of the promise, is evident in the person, our Savior, Jesus the Christ (Hebrews 6:17 ESV).

Let us think of His imputed truth to us this way: both the Word of God and Christ are blameless (Hebrews 6:18 ESV). As written, it is impossible for God to lie (Hebrews 6:18 ESV). What is set before us as we learn of God is fulfilled in His Word, which we read, and this same Word has been given to us by the inspiration of His Spirit (Hebrews 6:18 ESV).

What we hold fast to is the imperishable Word of Truth, for in our hands, are we not such as the disciples, encouraged and given hope from both the words we read and what Christ has spoken (Hebrews 6:18, Luke 24:31–32 ESV)?

What was confirmed before the disciples who saw, listened to, and walked with the resurrected Christ remains with us. Now, as we read Scripture and experience the indwelling presence of Christ among us, our souls then yearn to confirm to one another.

> Did not our hearts burn within us while He talked to us on the road, while He opened to us the Scriptures? Luke 24:32

Therefore,

> every Word of God proves true; He is a shield to those who take refuge in Him. Do not add to His Words, lest He rebuke you and you be found a liar. (Proverbs 30:5–6)

Lord, as you open our eyes to recognize You in Your Word, help us gain the faith that Your Word activates our souls by Your truth. As for those bloodthirsty men who hated our Savior, the blameless one, let their guilt be upon them, while for us who believe, we live seeking after the life of the righteous one (Proverbs 29:10 ESV). Christ is our sure and steadfast anchor of hope that enters our souls as we meditate upon the teachings of Christ, who has gone before us, becoming a High Priest forever (Hebrews 6:19–20 ESV). So that others may be saved, we then do not try to please everyone; instead, whom we seek to please must be Christ (1 Corinthians 10:33 ESV). His Book of

Life, which we hold in our hands and Christ secured for us with His sacrifice, has been purchased on our behalf. What we now hope to proclaim are the words of the apostle Paul.

> Imitate me as I imitate Christ.
> 1 Corinthians 11:1

> Just say the Word Lord that we may be healed. For such as you Lord we are all under the authority of our Father (Luke 7:7–8 ESV).

May we then marvel with You, Lord, at how Your Word, once spoken, transforms our lives in line with our Father's will (Luke 7:7–10). Amen.

What, then, this Word of Truth tells us is that all that occurred in recent times is from the LORD (1 Corinthians 10:1–4 ESV). Intending life to be good on this planet, we all live in Christ, who has overthrown the evil that began in the first days of creation (1 Corinthians 10:4–5, Genesis 3:6 ESV).

Although the LORD provided for His nation, God was not pleased with most of them (1 Corinthians 10:5 ESV).

What was written in the Bible is "These things took place as examples for us, that we might not desire evil as they did" (1 Corinthians 10:6 ESV). They (referring to those who saw all that the LORD God did in bringing them out of Egypt, then providing food and water for forty years) doubted God as they, God's people, traveled through the wilderness (Exodus 19:4 ESV). For us, then, take no further pleasure in sinning against the LORD, our God and Creator; for what you do by indulging in sin is what Christ died for, our sins (1 Corinthians 10:6–9 ESV).

The instructions are the same.

On whom the end of the ages has come, take heed lest anyone who thinks they stand fall into the same condemnation as those removed from the presence of the LORD prior to even our lives (1 Corinthians 10:11–12, Genesis 3:23 ESV).

It's not always what we do but what we don't do!

IT'S WHERE OUR WORDS COME FROM!

Typically, it is better to be considered a fool than for a person to open their mouth, for in speaking, they remove all doubt. At other times, our inactions would be better than action, as when Eve ate of the forbidden tree in the Garden of Eden; it would have been best if she had starved (Genesis 3:6 ESV).

> Trust in the LORD with all your heart, and do not lean on your own understanding. In all your ways acknowledge him. Proverbs 3:5–6

What we believe as true is that by His wisdom, what we see and live upon this Earth was established by God's understanding (Proverbs 3:19 ESV). And yet in a time where the LORD's long-suffering was so grieved, it was the LORD, by His knowledge, who put an end to idolatry by breaking open the foundations of this earth, as the depths of the springs from within (along with the rain from the clouds), flooded this same Earth (Proverbs 3:20, Genesis 7:11 ESV). Those who were created quickly departed from this earth.

In an instant, return to God!

Go back to what you knew and did before sin beset you (Proverbs 4:23; Genesis 2:10, 3:6 ESV). In an instant, return to God by not fleeing from the commands of the LORD; so stay and listen to the source of life—the words from the mouth of Christ (Proverbs 5:7 ESV). To avoid the pitfalls beneath your feet, cling to the ways of your youth, staying away from those of impure speech.

> Keep your way far from her house.
> Proverbs 5:8

Unless the enemy flees from you first, imitate Joseph by moving away from the wicked one (Genesis 39:1–23 ESV). How? By staying nearer to Christ than when you first believed.

We need You, LORD, to keep us reading Your divine Scripture lest in a moment, we become broken beyond healing (Proverbs 6:15 ESV). Reprove us into disciples of Christ who are becoming discipled of—then disciplined in—the way of life (Proverbs 6:23 ESV).

Give us not the desires of ourselves but the desires of Your pure heart (Proverbs 6:25 ESV).

What we need from You, God, is to bind our fingers to our Bibles; for in reading Your Word, You may write these holy words on the tablets of our hearts (Proverbs 7:3 ESV).

Use all things for your glory. May we say that this day, we have fled from sin. Now, Lord, we are before You, seeking to meet with you, for we eagerly have sought to gain insight. And this day, you have founded Your Word in our souls. So teach us how to pray, and give us a longing to read what has been written (Proverbs 7:15 ESV).

Chapter 24

Explained

> *All these things Jesus said to the crowds in parables; indeed, He said nothing to them without a parable. This was to fulfil what was spoken by the prophet: "I will open my mouth in parables; I will utter what has been hidden since the foundation of the world."*
> —Matthew 13:34–35

The fear of the Lord is hatred of evil (Proverbs 8:13 ESV). And so we pray, knowing, believing, and trusting that in Christ, we have been counseled by proven wisdom, from whom we gain insight. For us who believe, our strength is from the Lord (Proverbs 8:14 ESV). In this, we trust that God loves those who love Him, as those who seek within what has been written find life (Proverbs 8:17 ESV).

Oh, if someone had explained to Eve that the fruit of the Lord is better than gold, even fine gold, and that what God yields surpasses silver, Eve would have trusted in You, God (Proverbs 8:19, Genesis 3:6 ESV).

Oh, that she would have seen that God treasured her highly (Proverbs 8:21 ESV). For at the beginning of His work, God formed Eve as one of His first acts of old (Proverbs 8:22 ESV).

Even greater for us, just as with Eve, we may no longer claim any ignorance of what God has fashioned; for before Eve, before us, what is made and seen was brought forth by our Creator (Proverbs 8:23–31; Genesis 1:1–2:23 ESV).

"For whoever finds Me," says God, "finds life and obtains favor from the Lord" (Proverbs 8:35 ESV), while those who fail to inquire of the Lord, in their hatred of God, find death (Proverbs 8:36 ESV).

God is inviting you out of your ordinary, futile life to follow Him, as His imputed truth to us says, "Leave your simple ways, and live, and walk in the way of insight" (Proverbs 9:6 ESV).

As you are among those who receive instruction, become even wiser, as what you are taught from the only righteous one increases what you have learned, that:

> the fear of the Lord is the beginning of wisdom, and the knowledge of the Holy One is insight. Proverbs 9:9–10

The Words from our Savior is this fountain of life (Proverbs 10:11)!

What we believe in Christ leads us into life (Proverbs 10:16 ESV). We find it is pleasant to listen to the wisdom of the Lord (Proverbs 10:23 ESV). If eternal life is prolonged by fearing the Lord, then by all means, Lord, let us give reverence to You, our Creator, this day (Proverbs 10:27 ESV). Indeed, Lord, our hope of the righteous one—our Messiah—has been born (Proverbs 10:28; Luke 2:11, 16 ESV).

Chapter 25

ALL THINGS TOGETHER

Since there was a beginning of days in our world, it is with unending praise that, because of Christ, there is no end of life (Hebrews 7:3 ESV). To believe this is to then share Christ's grace, so we must become humble (Proverbs 11:2 ESV). And since Christ is alive, He is our hope, as our inheritance into heaven is of what existed before our world was formed (Proverbs 11:7 ESV).

Knowing this, we are to help others see the traps set before them; for if we love others, we see ourselves as whom God has set before others to keep them from trouble (Proverbs 11:8 ESV).

Therefore, we are to remain silent before the Lord while sharing the life of Christ with others (Proverbs 11:12 ESV). To keep yourself from living without God's guidance, surround yourself with an abundance of those who believe in Christ so they may counsel you in truth (Proverbs 11:14 ESV). Delight your habits in the blameless life of Christ, for the righteous one will deliver truth to you (Proverbs 11:20–21 ESV).

What, then, we can say in confidence is this:

> The desire of the righteous ends only in good.
> Proverbs 11:23

Knowing that Christ still lives by the power of an indestructible life (Hebrews 7:8, 16 ESV), we find, as we read His Word, He always lives to make intercession for us (Hebrews 7:25 ESV). What, then, is made known to others are the fruits of the ways of each person (Proverbs 14:14 ESV). While love and faithfulness belong to the prudent, those quick to accept believe all they hear without first considering how the Word of God is included in the matter (Proverbs 14:15, 22 ESV).

It is within Scripture we read of a man who rightly and timely applied the truth of God to his situation, saying, "How then can I do this great wickedness and sin against God?" Genesis 39:9

Teach us to consider our ways, Lord, for You have numbered our days.

> That which is, already has been; that which
> is to be, already has been; and God seeks what
> has been driven away. Ecclesiastes 3:15

In other words, there is nothing new under the sun. All things that happen this day have already occurred thousands of years ago (Ecclesiastes 1:9–10 ESV). For a generation passes away, and a new generation is born, while the earth is permitted to exist only until the end. And still, the Word of God remains forever (Ecclesiastes 1:4 ESV).

God was the one who did it (Genesis 39:22 ESV). For God was with Joseph, and all that the Egyptian master had was under Joseph as he became the overseer of his house and field (Genesis 39:1–5 ESV).

For both kinds of men, it is God who has put eternity into the heart of man. What remains for those who spend their lives searching the Scriptures is what God has done and how He has done it; in all God did, does, and has done is the mystery to the mind of those who take pleasure in this gift of God to search His Word by His Spirit (Ecclesiastes 3:11–13 ESV).

As we expound on God's Word, if there is any error on our part, we know that our advocate will use what has been shared for the better (1 John 1:5–2:6 ESV). God will use His Word to teach what He wants each of us to learn, so we must not fear to teach; rather, teach in all reverence to our Holy God of the Bible.

Christ's compassion is for those who weep,

>
> for those who have lost loved ones,
> they do not weep
> for those that are without loved ones,
> they do not weep
> for those with no loved ones,
> do not weep
> for those with no one to love,
> they do not weep
> some, do not weep for who they were to love.
> what then remains is;
> Christ' compassion is for those who weep!
> >Luke 7:13

Chapter 26

Given To Us

*God appointed a Son who has
been made perfect—forever!*
— Hebrews 7:28

*Now, the point in what we are saying is this…
In speaking of a new covenant, He makes the
first one obsolete. And what is becoming obsolete
and growing old is ready to vanish away.*
— Hebrews 8:1, 13

This the Lord set up, not man (Hebrews 8:2 ESV).

What we see and know is they serve as a copy and shadow of the heavenly things (Hebrews 8:5 ESV).

But as it is, Christ' eternal permanent ministry is better since "it" is entrusted to us by God through Christ' atonement (Hebrews 8:6 ESV).

The Lord Christ said He-Himself will put His laws into our minds, as His Word will remain in our hearts being these eternal souls, for He is our God (Hebrews 8:10 ESV).

IT'S WHERE OUR WORDS COME FROM!

Consequently, as the fulfillment of the Holy place within His being Christ is too Holy to mention (Hebrews 9:1–5, 10:5–7 ESV).

This is…for you. Hebrews 9:20

This, the Lord set up, not man (Hebrews 8:2 ESV).

What we see and know is that they serve as a copy and shadow of the heavenly things (Hebrews 8:5 ESV).

But as it is, Christ's eternal and permanent ministry is better since "it" is entrusted to us by God through Christ's atonement (Hebrews 8:6 ESV).

The Lord Christ said He Himself will put His laws into our minds and that His Word will remain in our hearts, being these eternal souls, for He is our God (Hebrews 8:10 ESV).

Consequently, as the fulfillment of the holy place within His being, Christ is too holy to mention (Hebrews 9:1–5, 10:5–7 ESV).

To serve the living God takes effort (Hebrews 9:14, 17, 20 ESV).

And then do you revere the Book itself? Hebrews 9:19

This is the blood of the covenant that God
commanded for you. Hebrews 9:20

Without the shedding of Christ's blood and without believing in Christ, there is no forgiveness for your sins (Hebrews 9:22 ESV).

Do not neglect to meet together; for if you do not meet with believers, who, then, will you spend your time with? Nonbelievers (Hebrews 10:25 ESV).

If you disbelieve in Christ, understand that it is a fearful thing to fall into the hands of the living God (Hebrews 10:31 ESV).

Any participation with Christ must then be performed in the Spirit (Philippians 2:1 ESV). Comfort one another—yes, encourage one another with blessings, as words from God strengthen us; for in doing all these things, let this be your prize: to attain the likeness of the mind of Christ (Philippians 2:2 ESV). Do and say things showing that the interests of others' needs are your priority (Philippians 2:3–4 ESV). Do all these things while remembering to gain the mind of God belongs to God alone, for we were created by Him—only to be like Him (Philippians 2:5–6 ESV).

And now we are becoming as those who are of the faith, as Christ remains alive, preserving our souls (Hebrews 10:39 ESV).

Chapter 27

Everyone

Hear, you deaf, and look, you
blind, that you may see!
—Isaiah 42:18

That we love because He first loved us!
—1 John 4:19

Believers, what the Word of God has written for us is to inform those of us who read these things that what has been given to us in the name of the Son of God is so that as we read, we may know that by believing in Christ, we will—after our days on this earth—know that we will have eternal life (1 John 4:1, 5:13 ESV).

Ask anything in faith according to His perfect will, and you may be confident that God hears the words you speak and even the thoughts within your mind (1 John 5:14 ESV). For how may God give to you unless it—the imputed truth—is asked for (1 John 5:14–15 ESV)?

So it is not I, but now the Lord God asks you again. This is what His Word has been formed into—a tangible and understandable format for you. So it is God who asks you this day, "Would you like to read together?"

*****

If we have learned anything yet, it is this: God and Jesus have already requested that their spirit be sent to live within us (1 John 5:15 ESV). God longs to speak with those whom He loves, for both have been born; our souls and His love are each the manifest presence of life within these treasures of clay that our Lord God formed from the ground (1 John 4:7–9; Genesis 2:7, 22 ESV).

Believer, if God so loved us, we also ought to love one another (1 John 4:11 ESV). While no one has seen God the Father, the attribute of His spirit is love—this we both know and are attaining through Christ (1 John 4:12–13 ESV).

The purpose of God giving us His Word is that we may believe in Jesus as our Savior, as it says,

> And we have seen and testify that the Father has sent His Son to be the Savior of the world. Whoever confesses that Jesus is the Son of God, God abides in him, and he in God. 1 John 4:14–15

Believer or nonbeliever, this we share in common: a stout word from a man under authority.

> "Lord, do not trouble yourself, for I am not worthy to have you come under my roof. Therefore, I did not presume to come to you," for he knew, the soldier was unworthy of Christ. "But say the word, and let my servant be healed. For I too am a man set under authority, with soldiers under me: and I say to one, 'Go,' and he goes; and to another, 'Come,' and he comes; and to my servant, 'Do this,' and he does it." Luke 7:8

IT'S WHERE OUR WORDS COME FROM!

The same love that the Father has had since creation, this same awestruck amazement to make even God marvel, was spoken as Christ said,

> I tell you, not even in Israel have I found such faith. Luke 7:9

In faith, we ask of You, Lord, that when our souls return to You, we may be found well, for Christ has made us and redeemed us (Luke 7:10). Amen.

Chapter 28

From Purpose

Our thanks be to God, who has given us victory through our Lord Jesus Christ. Believing His Word produces proper fellowship, then pray to God with willingness (1 Corinthians 11:13, 15:57–58).

What, then, is proper from a natural perspective is for all of creation to remain in the condition that God created, as God's intent is perfectly designed with a purpose (1 Corinthians 11:14–16).

Knowing the household of believers is to join together to glorify God, do your part to improve and build your faith upon like-mindedness (1 Corinthians 11:17 ESV).

O Lord, be gracious to us. Connect us to all we do this day for a godly purpose (Isaiah 33:2, 5–6 ESV). Be exalted, our Lord, our judge, our lawgiver, that we may tell others He will save us (Isaiah 33:5, 33:22 ESV).

Seek and read from the book of the Lord, for the mouth of the Lord has commanded. And His spirit has gathered them (Isaiah 34:16 ESV). Everyone is to submit to God, as even the head of Christ is God (1 Corinthians 11:3 ESV).

Take into consideration, as you hear the Word of God, that this knowing of Christ, this personal relationship with Christ, cannot be imitated, replicated, or bought.

Who would dare try to buy godliness, you ask?

For we thought that God has distributed His grace freely to anyone who will believe (1 Corinthians 9:9 ESV).

While this is true, so it is that some, both willingly and then others who become trapped in lies and deceit, will offer tainted money in seeking to find favor with the Lord (Acts 8:18–19; Luke 22:1–6, 22:47–53; Mark 14:10–11; Matthew 26:14–16, 27:3–10 ESV).

After sin, those who lead others to betray Christ only further put their shame upon you as you seek to reconcile your conscience. Do not return to evil men, for they will say to you,

> What is that to us? See to it yourself.
> Matthew 27:4

For us who believe offer all that you have to God knowing Christ's sword of truth is to bring people together (Luke 21:1–4 ESV)!

Since the point of the law of God is to instill reverence in the hearts of humanity, let us recall the pieces of silver that Judas threw back to those who offered him the bribe. This is so that we, too, may learn to value Christ above thirty pieces of silver (Deuteronomy 31:9–13; Matthew 27:3–10 ESV).

Revere Christ

Every person who prays with an unrepentant soul brings condemnation upon themselves (1 Corinthians 11:4 ESV). What is written below is from the prophecy foretold long before Christ's birth, given to those before us so that they might believe the Word of God (1 Corinthians 11:4; Matthew 27:9–10 ESV). What we will read soon began before this day, even before Judas dipped his hand in the dish with Christ, who was teaching His disciples about the Lord's Supper; and before this, Judas decided to betray Christ (1 Corinthians 11:27; Matthew 26:14–16, 23 ESV).

> Whoever, therefore, eats the bread or drinks the cup of the Lord in an unworthy manner will

be guilty concerning the body and blood of the Lord. 1 Corinthians 11:27

Father of Your Word, at this moment, set our minds upon Your Word, which is eternal. Amen.

> When morning came, all the chief priests and the elders of the people took counsel against Jesus to put Him to death. And they bound Him, led Him away, and delivered Him over to Pilate the governor. Then when Judas, His betrayer, saw that Jesus was condemned, he changed his mind and brought back the thirty pieces of silver to the chief priests and the elders, saying, "I have sinned by betraying innocent blood."
>
> They said, "What is that to us? See to it yourself."
>
> And throwing down the pieces of silver into the temple, he departed, and he went and hanged himself.
>
> But the chief priests, taking the pieces of silver, said, "It is not lawful to put them into the treasury, since it is blood money." So they took counsel and bought with them the potter's field as a burial place for strangers. Therefore, that field has been called the Field of Blood to this day. Then was fulfilled what had been spoken by the prophet Jeremiah, saying, "And they took the thirty pieces of silver, the price of him on whom a price had been set by some of the sons of Israel, and they gave them for the potter's field, as the Lord directed me." Matthew 27:3–10

Eleven out of the twelve disciples took hold of the cup and the bread with reverence for Christ, as they understood it was Christ who was inviting them to partake in eternal matters. Jesus was inviting

IT'S WHERE OUR WORDS COME FROM!

and investing His time on earth with His disciples, as written by the apostle Paul, who was not at this table yet became an apostle after Christ's ascension. Paul knew the point of being a disciple of the Lord, as he said,

> For I do not want to see you now just in passing. I hope to spend some time with you, if the Lord permits. 1 Corinthians 16:7

The difference in actually becoming a disciple of Christ has little to do with money, as time is all that God requires of your life on earth.

> Let a person examine himself, then, and so eat of the bread and drink of the cup. For anyone who eats and drinks without discerning the body eats and drinks judgment on himself. 1 Corinthians 11:28–29

In one of the books of the law of God given to us by Moses, the above account of how Christ was betrayed is mentioned. Again, Lord, teach us how to give reverence to You, Your Spirit, Your Son, and Your Word. Teach us now, we ask. Amen.

Judas was found slain by a rope, fixed by the devil himself (Deuteronomy 21:1; Matthew 26:14–16; 26: 24–25; 27:5 ESV).

> Then Satan entered into Judas called Iscariot, who was of the number of the twelve.
> Luke 22:3

Judas, unlike the rest of the disciples, though at one time was numbered among the twelve, never submitted to the yoke of servanthood to Christ (Deuteronomy 21:3 ESV). As the water was running from the vessel in Christ's hands, it was the Lord sitting among His disciples who said to Judas, "What you are going to do, do quickly," referring to Judas betraying Him (Deuteronomy 21:4; Luke 22:20–21; John 13:27 ESV).

Do you need to take a moment to allow the Holy Spirit to reassure you that it—indefinite torment—is for Judas and not for you (Matthew 26:24)?

Chapter 29

UNITY

Father, bring me into Your Word.

> Then the priests, the sons of Levi, shall come forward, for the Lord your God has chosen them to minister to Him and to bless in the name of the Lord, and by their word, every dispute and every assault shall be settled. Deuteronomy 21:5

The dispute has nothing to do with anyone other than Christ and His instituting the ways of God into His Church (Luke 22:14–19 ESV). As Jesus said, "I have earnestly desired to eat this Passover with you before I suffer" (Luke 22:15 ESV).

The dispute is about Christ.

O Lord, accept Christ's life as the atonement for our sins. As included with those of Your people Israel, we, whom you have redeemed, are unworthy of the blood of Christ, which was shed for the remission of our sins. As You purged Judas from Your midst, yes, Lord, purify us with Christ's sacrifice. Let it be said this day that Christ's innocence has atoned for our iniquities.

Teach us to do what is right in Your sight, Lord (Deuteronomy 21:5–9 ESV).

For those such as Judas, who are accursed in their own dealings with lies, let their sin be upon them (Deuteronomy 21:22–23 ESV). Examine our souls before we eat and drink at Christ's table, "for anyone who eats and drinks without discerning the body eats and drinks judgment on himself" (1 Corinthians 11:28–29 ESV). This misuse of involving yourself in the Lord's Supper with unrepentant souls is what leads to illness (1 Corinthians 11:30 ESV).

> That is why many of you are weak and ill, and some have died. 1 Corinthians 11:30

The concern is not a dispute of who is the greatest, for the cup of salvation belongs to Christ alone. Christ gives us this participation in His sacrifice so as we are judged by the Lord, we are disciplined to become His disciples, not condemned (1 Corinthians 11:32 ESV).

> But when we are judged by the Lord, we are disciplined so that we may not be condemned along with the world. 1 Corinthians 11:32

> And they began to question one another, which of them it could be who was going to do this. A dispute also arose among them, as to which of them was to be regarded as the greatest. Luke 22:23–24

Are you aware the devil goes before the LORD, disputing to God whom Satan may be allowed to afflict?

> Now there was a day when the sons of God came to present themselves before the LORD, and Satan also came among them. The LORD said to Satan, "From where have you come?"
>
> Satan answered the LORD and said, "From going to and fro on the earth, and from walking

up and down on it." So Satan went out from the presence of the LORD. Job 1:6–11

God tells us all these things so that we may believe before His judgment is final. Remember what was said by the rich man tormented in hell: "Go send others to tell my loved ones of this impending torment that they may be saved" (Luke 16:27–28 ESV).

And the LORD's reply was, "If they do not hear Moses and the Prophets, neither will they be convinced if someone should rise from the dead" (Luke 16:31 ESV).

So it was in Luke 16:19–31:

> There was a rich man who was clothed in purple and fine linen and who feasted sumptuously every day. And at his gate was laid a poor man named Lazarus, covered with sores, who desired to be fed with what fell from the rich man's table. Moreover, even the dogs came and licked his sores. The poor man died and was carried by the angels to Abraham's side.
>
> The rich man also died and was buried, and in Hades, being in torment, he lifted up his eyes and saw Abraham far off and Lazarus at his side. And he called out, "Father Abraham, have mercy on me, and send Lazarus to dip the end of his finger in water and cool my tongue, for I am in anguish in this flame."
>
> But Abraham said, "Child, remember that you in your lifetime received your good things, and Lazarus in like manner bad things; But now he is comforted here, and you are in anguish. And besides all this, between us and you a great chasm has been fixed, in order that those who would pass from here to you may not be able, and none may cross from there to us."

And he said, "Then I beg you, father, to send him to my father's house—for I have five brothers—so that he may warn them, lest they also come into this place of torment."

But Abraham said, "They have Moses and the Prophets; let them hear them."

And he said, "No, father Abraham, but if someone goes to them from the dead, they will repent."

He said to him, "If they do not hear Moses and the Prophets, neither will they be convinced if someone should rise from the dead."

Have you received Christ?

Chapter 30

Connected

*No one can say "Jesus is Lord"
except in the Holy Spirit.*
—1 Corinthians 12:3

How, then, that nonbelievers have yet to profess Christ as Lord of their life lies in this spiritual matter: to say Jesus is Lord of your life must be done with the indwelling of the Holy Spirit (1 Corinthians 12:3 ESV).

If you lack anything from the Lord, such as salvation, ask for it—His internal truth into your soul—and the Father will promptly let your request be made known with your own words that confess Christ as Lord.

Ask for mercy so that the Lord may offer forgiveness to you.

In joining together to build a tower to heaven, those who began to multiply on the earth in the days following the world flood did not know the recompense from dishonoring the language of God's Word to them (1 Corinthians 14:11; Genesis 11:5–6 ESV). Therefore, the one who speaks His Word is true before and after in making foreigners of anyone who constricts what has been written (1 Corinthians 14:11 ESV). If God created many languages from one, then His inerrant text is meant to teach and warn us that if we do not live in obedience to the language of heaven now, what makes us think we will be welcomed into The Kingdom of God after our life on earth?

What was written by men is implied for eternity.

> Behold, they are one people, and they have all one language, and this is only the beginning of what they will do. And nothing that they propose to do will now be impossible for them.
> Genesis 11:6

For within every person is an eternal soul that knows, without professing, that it will exist forever. To remain with the Lord in the hereafter, give reverence to His Word in what we say and do.

Since the Tower of Babel, there are countless languages that God made since and after, as Genesis retells us of the flood—of how humanity's continual disobedience of not dispersing from one area to inhabit the earth—God brought confusion into a once unified people (Genesis 11:1–9; 1 Corinthians 14:10–11 ESV).

As mankind forsook the commands of the Lord, though they excelled in building a tower to heaven, God was not pleased (1 Corinthians 14:12; Genesis 9:2, 11:4 ESV).

Unless believers are eager to please the Lord, their Creator, in obedience to His Word, the Lord will interpret their actions as violating His commands (1 Corinthians 14:13 ESV). For those who are proud and those who doubt, is it not the Lord our God who has made man's tongue for the purpose of proclaiming the gospel (1 Corinthians 14:14; Exodus 4:11–12 ESV)?

> Once you get there, don't forget that "I AM" sent you!
> Exodus 3:14

Men say,

> What am I to do? 1 Corinthians 14:15

> Who am I that I should go to Pharaoh and bring the children of Israel out of Egypt?
> Exodus 3:11

IT'S WHERE OUR WORDS COME FROM!

God said,

> And they will listen to your voice, and you and the elders of Israel shall go to the king of Egypt and say to him. Exodus 3:18

Men say,

> But behold, they will not believe me or listen to my voice, for they will say, "The Lord did not appear to you." Exodus 4:1

> Oh, my Lord, I am not eloquent, either in the past or since you have spoken to your servant, but I am slow of speech and of tongue.
> Exodus 4:10

God said,

> Who has made man's mouth? Who makes him mute, or deaf, or seeing, or blind? Is it not I, the Lord? Now therefore go, and I will be with your mouth and teach you what you shall speak.
> Exodus 4:11–12

Where the spirit of the Lord is, hope remains!

Let's search the Word of God and try to apply the authority of both the voice of Christ and the Word of the Living God.

> Then He [Jesus] came up and touched the bier, and the bearers stood still. And He [Jesus] said, "Young man, I say to you, arise." And the dead man sat up and began to speak.
> Luke 7:14–15

What causes a man to rise to life from the dead? The Word of Christ!

Where else can we find the authority of Scripture and of God? In Christ, all things are complete, for ingrained truth tells us,

So now faith, hope, and love abide; these three; but the greatest of these is love (1 Corinthians 13:13 ESV).

> Where there is faith,
> Where there is hope,
> Where there is love; There is the eternal Christ!
> As all these things are given to us from God.
> 1 Corinthians 13:13

Again, Christ brings hope to others.

> Lord, if you had been here, my brother would not have died. But even now I know that whatever you ask from God, God will give you.
> John 11:21–22

God is predetermined to speak through and work through anyone who is willing! The same spirit of God lives in each person who claims Jesus's voice as greater than their own.

Chapter 31

REMAIN

The following are Christ's words.

> Be very careful, therefore, to love the LORD your God. For if you turn back and cling to the remnant of these nations remaining among you and make marriages with them, so that you associate with them and they with you, know for certain that the LORD your God will no longer drive out these nations before you, but they shall be a snare and a trap for you, a whip on your sides and thorns in your eyes, until you perish from off this good ground that the LORD your God has given you.
>
> Joshua 23:11–13

Christ's farewell was with His words to the Father.

> I glorified you on earth, having accomplished the work that you gave me to do. And now, Father, glorify me in your own presence with the glory that I had with you before the world existed.
>
> John 17:4–5

And to us, His disciples, Christ acknowledges us before the Father by saying,

> Sanctify them in the truth; your word is truth. As you sent me into the world, so I have sent them into the world. And for their sake, I consecrate myself, that they also may be sanctified in truth.
> John 17:17–19

The power, the authority, the truth, the excellencies, the inerrancy, and the infallible truth of Scripture exist because it was given to us by the Holy Spirit. The anointing on the Word of God—in the collection of events, conversations, and stories—tells us all that God, in His dominance, goodness, and glory, seeks to reveal to us that His Word is life! His Word is eternal and indestructible. Study, seek, and you will find His Word is true; for blessed are those who walk in the ways of the Lord, as within their minds is the law of the Lord. Therefore, unending praise belongs to the Lamb of God—Christ (Psalm 1:1–2 ESV).

Afterword

WHAT IS ETERNAL?

*Jesus Christ is the same yesterday
and today and tomorrow!*
—Hebrews 13:8

In all that Jesus did and began to do, Jesus taught His disciples the Word of God must go forth to accomplish the Will of the Father. Whoever seeks the Lord gains insight into God's Word, for little by little, God brings the increase (Proverbs 13:11 ESV).

So by all means, live expecting Christ's return; for as the Lord sent Moses in a thick cloud, that the people might hear God speaking to Moses, we as well are to live consecrated, holy lives both today and tomorrow (Exodus 19:1–11 ESV). The time is already upon us in that Christ arose on the third day (Luke 24:1–7 ESV).

Has it been forever since you believed in Christ? Or will this day be the first among many days where you believe in Christ eternally (Exodus 19:9)?

Forgive, and you will be forgiven.

> If your enemy is hungry, give him bread to eat, and if he is thirsty, give him water to drink, for you will heap burning coals on his head, and the LORD will reward you. Proverbs 25:21–22

What we share of Christ—one with another—is then meant to further the gospel, for all people except Christ have sinned and fallen short of the glory of God (1 Peter 3:14–18; 1 John 1:8 ESV). Teach us then, LORD, to let our yes be yes and our no be no, for everything else is from the devil (James 5:12 ESV).

Lord, I believe; help my unbelief. Teach me how to apply Your Word as the instructions of my soul. Put me before those who speak truth this day (John 20:27; Proverbs 23:12 ESV).

For it is my Lord who has given me life, life from the Holy Spirit, who teaches me to listen to the Father! What the spirit of God says is this ancient wisdom of life (Proverbs 23:22 ESV). Include my soul with Your spirit, Your Son, and You, LORD, for in the abundance of Your counsel is eternal truth (Proverbs 24:6 ESV).

Instruct me as Your Word is before me this day, and as I read, teach me, I ask. Amen.

> If we say we have no sin, we deceive ourselves, and the truth is not in us. 1 John 1:8

> In your hearts, honor Christ the Lord as holy, always being prepared to make a defense to anyone who asks you for a reason for the hope that is in you; yet do it with gentleness and respect, having a good conscience, so that, when you are slandered, those who revile your good behavior in Christ may be put to shame. 1 Peter 3:15–16

Christ's love may abide in you!

> As the Father has loved me, so have I loved you. Abide in my love. John 15:9

From the author, the spirit of the living God,
This is what has been developed by God by His Word for years. This book is all from God developing through His Bible-reading plans with my sons and I, who through FaceTime and phone calls

IT'S WHERE OUR WORDS COME FROM!

pray, read, talk about what we have read, and then pray again. This book is a confirmation of scripture of my sons and I being led by God as we read His Word on a nightly routine. As life interrupts when we miss days or weeks, we keep reading where we last read.

This book is the overflow of the Holy Spirit being pleased with us reading His Word as God is in our personal reading plan. This book began with my sons and I reading plan and my personal reading plan with God. This was motivated by my years of online classes at Liberty University, of years of attending church without my family, and how faith was brought forth from reading God's Word one word at a time. What remains after attending weekly men's Bible studies and a prayer group is this yearning to do more with God and for God.

This began on Thursday, May 18, 2023, when God had me to begin a personal prayer journal with Him and His Word. In reading and listening to sermons, messages, songs, and anything and everything one word and one page at a time, God began this discipline within me of reading, writing, and praying these words of God with God, mostly for my wife, sons, and I, then recording these now two prayer journals of some 115 pages by reading them out loud and recording them on my phone.

Then as of December 15, 2023, with my course completed and submitted on my last day to complete my Bachelor of Science Religion: Biblical and Theological Studies from Liberty University. At work as a builder/carpenter in my truck during break, needing to start another New Testament book with God to join with my personal reading of Isaiah, God brought me to begin reading 1 Corinthians 1:1. That day after work, knowing the presence of Christ wanted my wife and me to read His Word together, with no response from my wife, I texted on December 9, 2023: "I've been thinking about you and I reading a book of the Bible together. Any book you would like to read with me? I'm available now to read if you are led. You may call, and we could read for a moment."

I texted my wife, telling her I read what God urged me to read twice, yet without us both reading, this is incomplete. Though my wife and I did not begin reading together, these words in this book were brought forth by a moving of the Holy Spirit this eternal love from God to my wife, sons, and I. My wife and I said few words to each other in some eight years.

This book is an effort to allow the Spirit of God, of Christ, to have His way in our lives, to act in faith of our living God by studying His Word! Knowing that my wife and I were commissioned by God to read together, the Holy Spirit remains active in my family. What began as two weeks has now become one book written in a few weeks. After a year, this book is brought to you to lead you by the Holy Spirit to read scripture with others and with God. What God had for me to write with Him, the Author of Life, is meant for you to read.

This book is inspired of His Word, for His Word, by His Word.

In asking for help by emailing churches and radio stations, this book began with a moving of the Holy Spirit, an awareness of God's presence, and an assurance that God is for my family! These words give back an acknowledgment of how God anoints our time spent in Bible reading plans, particularly my sons and I being taught directly by the Holy Spirit!

The conversations my sons, God, and I have are proof of God's amazing Spirit of grace! In needing and wanting a chance to do more with God for God, Christian Faith Publishing is giving my family this chance.

This book is from this mindset: "For what would we say without the Word of God!" God is encouraging you to read His Word!

Reading with my sons is mostly done over the phone, FaceTime. We pray and read, and God has me ask my sons questions like "What does this mean?" and "Who is this person?" We talk about God's Word and include our lives in it, then we pray, again my sons pray, and I pray. God is teaching us how to become disciples of Jesus Christ.

All of this is possible in commune with my sons and with our God!

What has become of our Bible-reading plan is my sons each asking me daily, "Will you read to me?" A week ago, in starting the book of Revelation, one of my sons read the title, and my other son read a few verses. Now, as of last night, January 12, 2024, my oldest

IT'S WHERE OUR WORDS COME FROM!

son read four verses out loud as I held my phone over our Bible from Iowa to my sons in Arkansas. The Holy Spirit is with us and for us!

The question God asks you is, "Do you want to read together?"

By faith we understand that the universe was created by the Word of God, so that what is seen was not made out of things that are visible.
—Hebrews 11:3

About the Author

About the Author the Spirit of our living Creator,

"For, what would we say without the Word of God!" Is the mindset of writing, *It's Where Our Words Come From!*

This book is about the Holy Spirit discipling us from His Word for His Word. Years of consistently praying and reading scripture with my sons is bringing us closer to Christ. The Holy Spirit speaks forth life as we pray, read, as we talk about our LORD's Word giving encouragement to us as our faith is in the name of Christ Jesus our Lord and Savior.

This book is written from our personal Bible reading plan. How we begin our time in the Word is with my sons saying - will you read to me!

This book is motivated by years of online classes at Liberty University, by God's love for us, with a passion for Christ's church; God teaches us.

Love from God is shared in fellowship with my sons; faith is brought forth from God's Word; doctrine is taught by Liberty University.

In Christ our study of scripture is ongoing. My eternal accomplishment of discipling my two sons who are my lifelong degree completion plan gave me a want to complete my Bachelors of Science and Theological Studies from Liberty University in 2023.

This Book is inspired of His Word, for His Word, by His Word!

IT'S WHERE OUR WORDS COME FROM!

This book is written with God's eternal love for my wife and sons.

This is an effort to allow the Spirit of God, of Christ to have His way in our lives! To act in faith of our living God by studying His Word! God anoints the conversations my sons and I share with God giving life and hope to our souls as we are taught directly by the Holy Spirit!

God is teaching us how to become disciples of Jesus by communing with his Spirit. Scripture is our structure of discussion as God leads my sons and I with questions: "could you explain this to me?" We talk about God's Word and find our life's hope in scripture, we pray my sons pray and I pray. One instance we began the Book of Revelation with my

youngest son reading the title, "Revelation" and my oldest son reading the first verses of Revelation chapter 1.

God yearns for you to ask others;

"Do you want to read together?"

Christian Faith Publishing is giving your family
this chance to study Jesus Christ.